—at any Cost?

MARY MEALYEA

KINGSWAY PUBLICATIONS
EASTBOURNE

First published 1987

ISBN 0 86065 450 8

Front cover photo: Tony Stone Photolibrary – London

Printed in Great Britain for
KINGSWAY PUBLICATIONS LTD
Lottbridge Drove, Eastbourne, E. Sussex BN23 6NT by
Cox & Wyman Ltd, Reading.
Typeset by CST, Eastbourne, E. Sussex.

Contents

TO
HARRY

Author's Note

There is a very familiar story which I have always found helpful. It's about three Chinese men who were walking along the great wall of China. One was called Fact, another Faith and the third Experience. Fact walked along first with Faith following behind and Experience taking up the rear.

Whenever Faith had his eyes firmly fixed on Fact in front of him he was fine. However, when he turned round to examine Experience he fell off the wall.

Sometimes we do have our eyes firmly fixed on the facts of God's love and we do believe with our minds that he loves us and that his plans for us are good and perfect. But in our hearts all we feel is pain, and we cry out, 'Yes, Lord, I *know* that you love me but sometimes I don't *feel* like it.'

Similarly, when we consider our childlessness we know that this is not a punishment given to us by a sadistic God. However, sometimes deep down our hearts cry out, 'Lord, what have I done? Why have you withheld this precious gift and blessing from me?'

A short time ago I was reading the book *Five Evangelical Leaders* by Christopher Catherwood (Hodder & Stoughton 1984). I was interrupted just as I was reading about James Packer and it was some days before I was able to return to it. As I was opening the book to find the place, I remember thinking to myself, 'Why is it these people don't ever suffer from infertility? They all seem to be blessed with large, happy families.'

The first words I read were these: 'The Packers have three (adopted) children.'

I realized afresh that God is no respecter of persons. It's not a question of being good or bad, gifted or ungifted, reward or punishment. To see that someone whose ministry God had obviously blessed could be subject to some of the same hurt that we had experienced, brought comfort to my heart as well as rebuke to my self-pity. I was reminded too of that great evangelist, pastor and hymn-writer of the eighteenth-century—John Newton—who with his wife longed for children but had none.

Being able to identify, even in a little way, with others perhaps whom God has blessed and whose ministry has brought blessing to others, can comfort us. For those of us who consider ourselves very ordinary Christians this can be a source of tremendous encouragement to press on.

As I pondered all this in my heart I wondered if perhaps even a few people like ourselves could be helped, comforted and encouraged by my sharing our own story.

Dr Packer has very kindly written a few words of commendation of my book and I am grateful to both him and his wife Kitty.

Foreword

A missionary bishop once told me how he and his wife had construed their childlessness as God setting them free to take the whole young church as their family. I thought this heroic, for childlessness starts as desolating disappointment. The desire to give one's spouse children as well as pleasure is deeply rooted, and the pain felt by infertile couples, wives in particular, is great, as Scripture itself shows.

Ray Mealyea traces this with honesty and realism, bravely opening her own grief in order to relieve the bottled-up grief of others. My wife, who was once where Ray is, and a friend who is there now, have read the book and found it good, and their commendation must be held to count for more than mine.

In *A Severe Mercy* Sheldon Vanauken tells how C. S. Lewis rebuked him for not realizing, as Elkanah before him also failed to realize, what childlessness can do to a loving wife, and I feel that I too am limited here. Gladly, however, do I let the world know that two witnesses who have a right to speak give Ray Mealyea's book highest praise, and that I do the same.

J. I. Packer

Acknowledgements

I want to acknowledge my debt to a number of people who have helped me in the writing of this book: to Harry my husband who encouraged me to write it—it was his confidence in me that enabled me to get started; to Dr Anne Townsend without whose practical help and encouragement, and editing, it would probably never have reached the publisher; also our good friend Eric Wright for his careful reading of the manuscript and helpful comments. And finally my thanks to Frances Davies and Rosemary Kent of Care Trust who typed the manuscript.

Introduction

'Why not write a book about it?' Little did I realize that my wife would take me seriously. We had been discussing for perhaps the umpteenth time in our ten years of marriage an issue which had brought sorrow and vexation into our personal lives—our childlessness. During those years we had struggled to come to terms with a whole host of feelings: inadequacy, failure and unfulfilment, not to mention those strong maternal drives and mothering instincts which baffled husbands can only begin to imagine.

It did not take us long to discover that childlessness is one of those taboo subjects which are rarely sensitively or honestly dealt with in Christian fellowships. We were fortunate in being able to share our plight with a few sensitive and understanding friends, but by and large the subject tends to be skirted in conversation or approached in a quite heartless manner. What a tremendous pressure there is to become a Christian 'clam', refusing to be prised open lest emotionally sensitive nerve endings are touched or lest our psychological hang-ups and feelings of abnormality be exacerbated. We found that others' casual throw-away remarks had a profoundly irritating quality, like the grain of sand within the sensitive shell. Initially we were happy to leave this subject firmly closed.

It did not, however, take us long to realize that our silence was contributing to the taboo. Our silence did little to argue for the necessity of understanding care and support. This book is part of a determined effort to open the clam and to break the taboo. It is not designed to feed the idly curious, but attempts to foster an understanding of a delicate subject which merits exposure. This sort of exposure is always costly. It is not unlike walking an emotional tightrope; aware of the dangers of disclosing more information about a marriage than is necessary, the cost of sharing failures and failings and bringing them into public view. For a long time Ray wrestled with the idea that she might write under a pseudonym. This would certainly have eliminated all fear of candour and would have avoided costly exposure. But we both eventually came to the conclusion that to have done so would merely have served to strengthen the taboo from which we sought to break free.

This book is not merely the product of the experience of one childless couple. During the years of our own childlessness we have been able to talk with many others in similar circumstances. We have entered into one another's sorrows, shared the grief of being misunderstood, encouraged those suffering from unsympathetic treatment from family and friends, and sought to comfort the baffled and sore in heart. The result of this travail has given birth to the book before you. We hope and pray that it will be a means of support and encouragement to the childless and a means of stimulating sensitivity among friends of the childless. I believe that this book attempts to show that childlessness need not be viewed as second rate, but something which God can use quite gloriously and positively. Indeed he is able to take the irritating grains of sand and from them produce a wonderful pearl of Christian character.

H. B. Mealyea

1

Initial Feelings

A few simple words possessed the power to throw me into a sudden downward spiral of depression and self-pity.

Certain questions I struggled to avoid would flood into my mind yet again. I'd find myself praying: 'Why Lord? It seems so easy, *too* easy, for other people to have babies. Would I be such a failure as a mother that you couldn't trust me with a baby? Heavenly Father, why won't you answer my prayers and give me the child for which I long?'

It had been simple words—the kind people said almost every day—that had had this effect on me. 'Have you heard Irene's news? She's expecting in April. She always wanted a Spring baby. Isn't it wonderful!'

It *was* wonderful, and I knew it was. Yet words like those knifed my heart as I struggled to smile and reply—really meaning what I said: 'Yes that's lovely!' I hoped the speaker would neither detect the anguish hidden behind my smile nor notice my eyes brimming over with tears.

If you are one of those who suffer from infertility then you will know exactly what I am writing about. You may be feeling happy and content—even congratulating yourself on how well you are coping with your personal disappointment—when a few casual words unexpectedly throw you off balance.

About ten to fifteen per cent of couples are reckoned to experience some degree of difficulty in having children, resulting in 'sub-fertility clinics' overflowing with childless couples seeking medical help.

Statistically it was reckoned in 1984 that there were one million childless couples in the United Kingdom. (Child Chat Newsletter, April–June 1984.)

It has been said that

> the condition of infertility is usually traumatic for the sufferers. Nobody is ill with it or usually dies from it. It's an invisible but devastating disability. For couples it challenges their role as procreators, their masculinity and femininity; it results in feelings of incompleteness, guilt and deep unhappiness. (Child Chat Newsletter, July–September 1984.)

Heartache

How do Christian couples cope if they face an agonizing situation like this?

How do you cope with all the different emotions that rise to the surface of your mind when you face the devastating realization that you may not be able to have any children of your own? Is it right to seek medical help, and if you do then how long should you persist and to what lengths should you go?

How do you exercise a vital faith in God when you live with an undercurrent of heartache and disappointment? How can you begin to accept that denial of the precious and legitimate gift of children comes from the hand of a *loving* heavenly Father, who desires only the best for you?

How do you learn to live contentedly, despite dashed hopes and shattered dreams? Can anyone really be joyful and fulfilled if they do not have children?

I went to medical school in 1970 to train to be a doctor. I had wanted to be a doctor for as long as I could remember and my ultimate goal was to be a medical missionary. Part of my medical course involved me in seeing and dealing with patients in most of the specialities. So inevitably I saw women in the gynaecology wards, some of whom were there for investigation and treatment of infertility. I had heard all about the subject in my lectures and studied it in my text books but it never entered my head that one day I myself would be classed as 'infertile' (or 'barren' as the Bible calls it). I had considered the possibility that I might never get married and might have to stay single, but I loved babies and children and always assumed that if ever I married I would automatically produce a large happy family.

Now, after ten years of marriage (which includes six years, on and off, of undergoing infertility investigations and treatment, plus two miscarriages), finally I am forced to face the reality that having children of my own is extremely unlikely.

I have found the burden of infertility a heavy load to carry, and I can now see that at times I have given myself a great deal of unnecessary pain by failing to handle the situation in the best way. Yet through years of hurt and tears—so many tears—I have been conscious of God's comforting arms around me. He has sheltered me in the pain I found almost unbearable. His arms have been underneath me, carrying me, when I could no longer cope in my own strength. He has then taken me by the hand and gently led me forward in what I believe to be his good and perfect will for my life. Looking back over these years I am now able to sense that God has given me gifts even more precious than his gift of children. He has helped me to know him more deeply, and he is also changing me and amazingly making me more like Jesus.

God has helped me handle my grief and incredibly has enabled me to *rejoice* through the pain. I hope that by sharing with you, you will be encouraged and able to avoid some of the mistakes I made. If you already have children then I trust this will help you as you get to know some who long for children of their own but are infertile.

Miscarriage

I met Harry, an architect, while I was still a student and we fell in love. We were both relieved to discover that we shared the desire to go abroad to do missionary work.

Apart from our natural desire to get married sooner rather than later, we felt it would be good to have been married a year or two before embarking on a completely different sort of life in a strange country. As we hoped to go abroad immediately after my year as a house officer, which corresponded with Harry finishing a three year course at Bible college, we decided to get married just before my final year as a medical student. So if I was going to finish training as a doctor and complete my house jobs contraception was essential. So I went on 'the pill' but hated it and often forgot to take it because in my heart of hearts I really wanted a baby. At last the time came when we thought that even if I did get pregnant I could still finish my residency year as a doctor. So I stopped taking the pill.

Before I took the pill my periods had always been regular, but when I stopped taking it they never returned to their normal pattern again. This was difficult because each time my period was late (as it often seemed to be) I was convinced that at last I must be expecting a baby.

Five or six months after stopping the pill my period again did not start when it was due. I had a pregnancy test—and to my delight and amazement it came back positive. But joy and expectation were short-lived. Three weeks after the test I began to miscarry. When I got over my immediate disappointment, I comforted myself with the fact that at least I knew I *could* conceive. As a doctor I knew that a fairly high percentage of first pregnancies miscarry with the majority of women going on to carry babies to full term later. As we were planning to go out to Iran within the next few months I had plenty to keep my mind occupied.

But two years later thoughts like these lost their power to comfort me. We had not used birth control for two years yet still I was not pregnant. I began to feel concerned and worried. The revolution in Iran had reached its peak and with the arrival of Khomeni we were obliged to return home to Scotland.

Eventually, I mustered sufficient courage to make an appointment to see a gynaecologist and he arranged some investigations. I had a D & C (dilatation and curettage) to check that the lining of my womb was normal. I also had a tubal insufflation where air is blown into the fallopian tubes and pressure readings on graph paper indicate whether the tubes in which the eggs and sperm travel are clear or not.

The gynaecologist reassured me that everything was all right. 'Don't worry,' he reassured me, 'you'll soon conceive again.' It was important for me to feel reassured, for anxiety about conceiving a baby can act as effective birth control for many women. The menstrual cycle is controlled by a small gland at the base of the brain called the pituitary gland which secretes various hormones. It is sensitive to stress and can even prevent the release of eggs—ovulation. When anxiety and stress over trying to conceive a baby are removed, then ovulation may take place and pregnancy occur. Tension can also cause spasms of the fallopian tubes. They clamp down and the husband's sperm are prevented from getting to the egg shed at ovulation from the woman's ovary.

Reduced horizons

I knew all of this from my training as a doctor and so I struggled to remain calm and placid, and to stop myself from *trying* to conceive. It was easier said than done!

One of the things I found hard to cope with at this time was those irregular periods of mine. But I now see that God had a valuable lesson for me to learn through it all. It took me a long time to realize that a woman who is repeatedly trying to have a baby lives with greatly reduced horizons. She often lives from one period to the next. Her world begins to revolve around waiting for the next period to start—or rather hoping that it won't.

I had fallen into this trap. My problem was made worse by the fact that my periods often arrived several weeks late and eventually became totally erratic. Every time the due date of my period came and passed, then hope began to rise.

I would try to talk sense into myself: 'Don't be silly, your period's often late.' Then I would argue: 'This time it *might* be different. I might be pregnant.'

Thinking that I *could* be expecting, I would begin to take things easy, in view of my previous miscarriage. 'Careful not to overdo things,' I'd tell myself and try to rest more than usual.

And then when the late period finally arrived my hopes crashed down, leaving me miserable and depressed. However, that depression and fear only lasted a few days, for hope would flicker to life again as I moved into the next cycle. 'Maybe next month!' I encouraged myself. And so it went on . . . month after month.

> There is no pain I know as crushing and potentially destructive as infertility, no human experience that every month for the rest of a woman's life, reminds her of the grief. The loss. The shattered dream. (Ann Kiemel Anderson in Vicky Love, *Childless Is Not Less*, Bethany House.)

Slowly I began to realize that this was having a profound effect on me. At times I must have been unbearable to live with. My life seemed to revolve around my periods and my longing for a baby. Yet I felt guilty as I knew that God did not intend me to live like this.

Hormonal changes

As I realized I had a problem and began to think it through, I saw that some of my emotional reactions were simply due to the hormonal changes going on inside me as part of a perfectly normal menstrual cycle. During this cycle the hormones oestrogen and progesterone rise, but just before a period starts they both fall to a base-line level.

Research has revealed that many women do not perform at their best in driving tests, exams, interviews and so on around the time of their period.

Many experience pre-menstrual tension (PMT)—a recognized syndrome—to varying degrees. Many are more tired and more easily upset at this time of the month than usual and some are irritable or even aggressive. Some suffer the effects of fluid retention. Some feel physically unwell just before and during the first few days of their period. The precise cause of all this is not fully understood but to some extent changing hormone levels are responsible. Whatever the cause, many women tend to be 'emotionally fragile' up to twelve days before the onset of a period.

For the woman who is trying to conceive, the disappointment of realizing that she is not pregnant coincides with the precise time in her cycle when she is most vulnerable. Her natural disappointment, coupled with her normal emotional response to a drop in hormone levels, can leave her feeling totally devastated.

Understanding all this helped me—especially in coping with my guilt at crumpling in a heap each time a period started. Eventually my husband and I were able to get it into sufficient perspective even to be able to joke about it. I would be sitting crying my heart out with disappointment yet at the same time laughing and saying: 'It's these silly hormones of mine again!'

Being human

At this stage I had to begin to learn how to accept my humanity and the effect that the normal functioning of my body had on my emotions. I was not Wonder Woman! I needed to recognize my feelings and to accept them for what they were. One of the things I had to accept was that I was disappointed and that I *was* feeling miserable partly because of PMT. At first it was not easy to accept these feelings without judging myself and thinking that my feelings made me a failure as a person! Gradually I was able to think it through and know that these feelings would not last—the sadness would pass in a few days.

As time went on and I learned to cope with monthly disappointment better, I gradually began to feel that I was indulging myself a little as I blamed everything on my hormones. All too easily they became an excuse for irritability, anger or distress. I found that whenever I flew off the handle at Harry or became ultra-sensitive over something trivial I would wait till I had calmed down and then apologize to my long-suffering husband with the words: 'But it's not really my fault. My period must be due, and I expect my hormones are playing me up!'

It was my husband who gently challenged me about this after some time, and God slowly indicated that he wanted to teach me another important lesson.

God wanted me to learn that he did not intend my life to be dominated either by the power of my body's responses to normal monthly hormones, or by the ensuing disappointment. Yes, I needed to recognize both for what they were. But recognition of these facts did not imply that they were to rule the way I lived. 'Surely,' I told myself, 'God can control me, and he is stronger than my hormones. Surely God does not intend me to be at the mercy of a constantly changing hormonal balance?'

At this stage I did not know that in fact my hormone balance was *abnormal,* and that this was making life even more difficult.

I started to pray specifically about the effect those hormones were having on me. I asked God to help me learn how to handle my emotions. Each time I realized I was pre-menstrual, I would pray particularly that God would help me and fill me with serenity and love. My problem did not disappear magically overnight. My periods have continued to be irregular apart from times when I have received infertility medicines. But God *has* helped me to cope better with the emotional side of the problem, and he has shown me that I should not use it as an excuse for being difficult to live with.

Even now, after many years, my heart still sinks with disappointment at the arrival of each period —despite the fact that I now know there is very little hope of my ever having a baby. However, I am now able to accept the disappointment and to ask God to hold me tight and safe until it has passed.

Facing problems

I believe that recognizing and facing problems, and then praying about them, is half the battle. After all, God intends Christians to learn and mature through life's painful experiences, and this is possible for us as we open ourselves up to receive his grace.

Once I had learned these initial lessons that God was teaching me, I naïvely thought that this would be an end to it. I assumed that I was over it. I could cope with having no children if that was what God had planned for me. Now I could put it all behind me and get on with life.

But it wasn't long before I fell flat on my face again. Once more something devastated me—I cannot even remember what it was. It may have been something like a close friend telling me she was expecting a baby. Whatever it was, it left me feeling a complete failure. Hadn't I learned how to cope with not being pregnant? I thought I had graduated beyond that stage. Yet, there I was, back at square one again.

Eventually I picked myself up, and tried to cope again. 'Right Lord,' I prayed, 'this time I really *do* accept the situation. I've put it behind me.' But each time it wasn't long before I was re-enmeshed in vulnerability, falling victim to yet another well-meaning friend's remarks.

I would cry about this, and try to explain to my husband: 'I seem unable to learn what God is trying to teach me. I thought I'd accepted God's purposes for me and was willing to go through with them, yet here I am breaking my heart again.'

Maternal instincts

All this helped me begin to understand from my own experience that a woman's maternal instincts are far too strong to be extinguished by the simplistic means I had tried. I could not brush those instincts to one side or sweep them under the carpet and say they would never bother me again. My longing for motherhood was something with which I was going to have to live.

Film star Susan Hampshire says of herself:

> The powerful biological urge to have a child is inexplicable. You can give someone a hundred reasons for not wanting a child, or not wanting more children, but the determination of a woman wanting a child will never be thwarted by rationalisation . . . I shall go on trying, possibly till my last period has come and gone when I know it's too late. (Susan Hampshire, *A Book for Every Woman Who Wants A Child,* Sphere.)

I even went as far as asking God to take away my maternal instincts if he intended never to give me children—for life would be easier without them. But God did not, and still has not, taken away that normal feminine desire implanted in women by their Creator.

I now expect to wage this war with myself for the rest of my child-bearing years. Each time a period starts I am reminded of my inability to conceive. Yet I no longer return to square one every time I lose a battle in this war. I am growing, and learning more about myself. I now understand my weakness better and see how much I need God's help. As time passes I am winning more and more of these battles. I have now learned how to recognize certain situations in which I am likely to be vulnerable to hurt and then either avoid them or pray my way through them.

I no longer expect myself to be able to cope with *every* sensitive situation.

I no longer tell myself: 'I've got over this completely. It's passed. It's not going to bother me any more.'

Rather I say: 'I'm learning, and with God's help

I'll be able to cope with more.' Each battle I win gives me confidence to go on. It still is a battle but I'm learning to draw on God's strength and resources. This is helping me a great deal.

Satan's ammunition

The devil is delighted when Christians are useless wrecks and paralysed by emotional turmoil. I am now beginning to recognize some of his fiery darts that have the potential to hurt me. These darts can be a few words which suddenly wound, and leave me very hurt. They can be the glimpse of a picture of a mother with a baby snuggling at her breast, emphasizing my sense of loss and emptiness. Such sudden happenings possess the power, in just a second, to switch my mood from one of contentment to despair and sorrow.

I believe these are all part of the ammunition the devil uses against God's children. As a Christian, I find it helpful that Paul commands us to 'take up the shield of faith, with which you can extinguish all the flaming arrows of the evil one' (Ephesians 6:16).

But how does this work out in practical terms? How do I cope when sudden attacks strike me off guard? I know I need to have a strategy for coping because these attacks will not evaporate. I also know that failure to handle them properly results in my sinking in a bog of self-pity.

Through such attacks I have begun to recognize that sometimes the devil is taunting me by making me think: 'God doesn't love me. If he *really* loved and cared for me, he would have given me a baby by now. He could easily work a miracle if that's what's needed. So, what's stopping him? It must be that he doesn't love me as much as he loves other people.' And for me the pain of thinking that God might not love me is even worse than that of being childless.

I have found that to recognize and grasp the fact that this kind of thinking is the devil's work helps me. I then know that such thoughts about God are not true. I know that the devil is a liar. So, I take up the shield of faith (spoken of in Ephesians 6) and hang on to what I know is the truth about God's character. I remind myself that God really does love me. I do not need to rely on any *feelings* about this for the Bible assures me of this *fact,* and the Bible tells the truth. I try to look back and remind myself of past experiences and evidences of how much God loves me. I have found that when I am able to do this, the sullen foreboding clouds of dark despair vanish.

I am not always successful though. There are times when I fail to recognize the devil's antics. I allow myself to listen to his lies, to believe them and to begin to be overwhelmed by self-pity. When this happens my darkness persists (sometimes as long as several days) until God breaks through with his light and reminds and reassures me that he *does* love me very much indeed. He understands my heartache, pain and bitter disappointment.

At times like this I tend to complicate the situation by feeling so guilty for having such negative thoughts about God that I am plunged into despair. But I regard this guilt reaction as the devil's counter-attack. Christians are engaged in spiritual warfare and their adversary has no rules. He sinks as low as is necessary to thwart God's plans for us, and so he makes particular prey of our weaknesses, striking us below the belt.

The fragile emotions of an infertile woman are easy targets for his arrows.

Rescued by God

When I fail God now (as I often do in this ongoing battle) I try not to waste energy and time by feeling guilty. I apologize to God for thinking such thoughts about him, and then I express my gratitude and praise to him for rescuing me and loving me so much that he stoops down to my level to turn my thoughts back to him and his goodness.

When I do this my peace and contentment are restored. God is teaching me how to handle the pain of infertility, and to recognize that he can turn even pain like this into something precious.

If I lived in a world isolated from other people then life might be plain sailing. As it is, I meet others daily, and not many realize how a thoughtless sentence can wound. Their words are still able to hurt me where I am vulnerable. Infertility is one of the few taboo subjects left in our culture, and most people are largely oblivious of the suffering and illness it can cause.

2

Anxiety

There was a time when it felt as if every time I met someone the first question I was bound to be asked was: 'Do you have any children yet?' I felt as if those words covered a deeper enquiry: 'If not, why not?' and the unspoken implication: 'Don't you think you should get a move on?'

Without even asking us, everyone seemed to assume that Harry and I had *chosen* not to have children. People's reactions ranged from almost accusing of us being selfish, to hinting that a lack of spiritual maturity was evident in our failure to understand that 'God wants you to have children'. Some said we were 'lucky' that we were not 'tied down by a family' and were 'free to serve the Lord fully'. One person, on finding out that we were childless, even suggested I would have found motherhood 'inconvenient' because of my career as a doctor!

Over the years I have had problems with my reactions to some well-meaning friends and acquaintances, and their thoughtless or insensitive comments.

Sense of failure

I recently read in Raymond Johnston's booklet for Care Trust on infertility that 'there is no sin or shame in being infertile'. Yet childless couples often feel ashamed and guilty about it. They ask themselves probing questions like: 'What wrong have we done in the past that makes us infertile?' Many of us sense shame and failure at a deep level. Coupled with this, we often feel we are not totally whole women or men.

Our intellect may tell us that there is no shame attached to infertility but our hearts deny this. My own experience is that this sense of shame and failure may be made worse (not better) by attitudes and thoughts of Christian friends. I know of one couple who were told that their infertility was 'due to unconfessed sin' in their lives. Months of heart-searching and agony followed as they thought of everything and sought God's forgiveness for it.

I have often thought that if I could be left alone in my own little world I would be happy and contented. But this is impossible. I cannot live in a vacuum. I live in a real world with real problems, and there is no way of escaping the realities which other people force on me. I cannot cut myself off in isolation.

Expectant mothers

Another difficult situation for me is when I find myself surrounded by expectant mothers who talk endlessly about their pregnancies. They say it is wonderful to feel the baby moving, and they discuss the kind of birth they want to have, when their baby is due, and what feeding programme they plan to adopt. I know it is natural and right for an expectant mum to be excited and to want to talk about her anticipated baby. But then some go on from this point to try to persuade me to 'take the plunge'. I dare not vocalize my thoughts: 'As if it were as simple as that!' I think people often talk like that without stopping to think: 'Could I possibly be hurting this person? Perhaps, just perhaps, she'd really like to have a baby like me—but she can't.'

With the best will in the world, I've found that at times Christian friends appear to be insensitive and uncaring because they have spoken on the assumption that I *could* have children. They have not looked at my face or sensed from my attitude that their words are misplaced.

Unfortunately the easiest way for people like me to react to this is to withdraw into a world of our own. We try to avoid all expectant mums and couples with children. But if we do that we then find ourselves lonely and isolated as one by one our friends join the category of 'those to be avoided because they are expecting or have children'.

There is no glib solution or easy answer to this problem. But I am sure the remedy does not lie in people like me erecting high barriers to distance ourselves from others. It would help a great deal if Christians, and non-Christians, were more aware of the problems of infertility. It would help if they knew about the deep personal hurt and disappointment which infertile couples suffer, and were more sensitive to their needs. Perhaps that will only happen when childless couples break the taboo of silence about infertility and are more able to share their feelings with their friends and relatives.

Sharing my secret

For several years I resisted talking to anyone except my husband about my unfulfilled desire to have a baby. I shrugged off questions like: 'When are you going to start a family?' I did not want anyone to know that I longed for children but seemed unable to have them, so I hugged my secret to myself. I preferred others to think we had *chosen* to be childless—it made me feel less of a failure. I also think I was afraid of being hurt by people's words probing what to me was a very sensitive issue. So I pretended the problem did not exist.

Finally, in my own interests, I had to break out of my self-imposed prison of silence and share with one or two close friends. I could no longer remain in isolation refusing to share myself with others.

I started by talking with Emily, a friend for many years. We had known one another before either of us had married and had shared one another's confidence for a long time. I felt safe with her and trusted her, so I invited myself round for coffee one morning. Soon I was pouring out the whole story hoping to find a sympathetic ear and helpful advice.

I was not prepared for her reaction. Emily had never sensed that we faced the problem of involuntary childlessness and like so many others had assumed we were still waiting for the 'right time' to start a family.

'Goodness,' she exclaimed without pausing to think, 'you're young and have plenty of time left to have a family. You've got yourself so worked up about it that I'm not surprised you can't conceive! Try to relax and forget it all . . . everything will work out in the end. Worrying won't help . . . anyway Christians are not supposed to be anxious. It's a bad witness for others to see you so distressed.'

As I walked home, my thoughts flew round and round in my head. I repeated the conversation over and over to myself. 'How could Emily be so insensitive? I'm older than she is—and she has two children already. She doesn't know what it's like for me. How would *she* cope if she were in my shoes? That's what I get for confiding in someone! I won't do it again!' I was angry and disappointed that my attempts to share had opened me up to even more hurt.

The wrong kind of anxiety

As I shared the conversation with my husband that evening I realized that I had overreacted to Emily's words. Yet I had a hunch there was an element of truth in what she said which challenged and disturbed me. It was the phrases 'Christians shouldn't be anxious' and 'It's a bad witness' that had struck me.

I think I am the sort of person who tends to worry too much over little things. My husband is the opposite and seldom gets anxious. While this is infuriating at times, we balance one another well to make a good team together. Emily's words sparked off a train of thought that helped me in many areas of my life as a Christian and not solely in the realm of infertility.

I thought hard about Jesus' teaching on the subject of worry and how he said: 'Therefore I tell you, do not worry about your life . . .' (Matthew 6:25–34).

The same word for 'worry' is used when Jesus reproached Martha: 'Martha, Martha . . . you are worried and upset about many things' (Luke 10: 41). She had no time for her guest. She was far too busy in the kitchen making sure her oven temperature was correct, being careful over the consistency of her scone mix and making sure her lamb kebabs were beautifully tender. Yet all the time she was missing the most important thing going on in her house that day—the ministry of Jesus.

I believe it is important to distinguish between legitimate concerns and unnecessary anxiety. It would have been wrong of Martha to neglect her guest's needs and to fail to provide him with a meal. But she was so absorbed in cooking that she forgot about the importance of spending time with her guest. Her anxiety was unnecessary, and her concern surpassed reasonable dimensions.

The anxiety which Jesus reproves has overtones of 'distraction by total absorption'. This helped me in thinking about my preoccupation and concern over being childless. When God created woman, he gave her a natural legitimate instinct to have children and to find fulfilment in motherhood. It is not wrong for a woman to desire to be a mother and to long for her own baby. However, legitimate concerns fuelled by the natural instinct of motherhood can push someone like me over the boundary fence and into the realm of such anxiety that it becomes a 'total absorption' which distracts us from other, more important, priorities.

'There is nothing like suspense and anxiety for barricading a human's mind against the enemy,' C. S. Lewis wrote in *The Screwtape Letters* (Fontana 1942, p.34) as advice was being given to a junior devil on how to stop a Christian from being effective in the service of God.

I have found that this kind of anxiety can so absorb me that it has the power of distracting me from Jesus. It not only debilitates me but it also reduces my ability to hear God's voice and to sense his reality. I know others who similarly have been crippled by anxiety, and whose lives have stopped running along the lines intended for them by God, because they were unable to discern God's guidance for them.

'Have I become totally absorbed in trying to have children?' I began to ask myself and tried to be honest with myself in reply. I saw other couples who were obsessed with trying to have a baby, to the exclusion of everyone and everything else. I had vowed that this would never happen to me. But had I, without realizing what was happening, allowed myself to be so anxious that it came into the category of 'distraction by total absorption'? Or was I dangerously hovering on the brink of being like that? These were hard questions to face frankly, but it helped me to be as ruthlessly honest with myself as I could be.

Insensitive

When someone like Emily glibly tells me 'Don't be anxious', the words not only demonstrate a lack of sensitivity and understanding but they do not really help at all. I know already that I should not be anxious. I know it would be a poor advertisement for Christianity if I was to be perpetually tense and worried. But I really needed someone to tell me how to handle my emotional anxiety rather than to tell me to stop something that I could not easily stop.

Those who conceive children easily and have had their maternal instincts satisfied know nothing of the strength and power of this instinct in driving a woman forward in her search to satisfy it. As I discovered, it is easy to cross over from the realm of legitimate concern into that of 'total absorption'.

As each month brought tears of disappointment I found my anxiety and tension mounting. Sexual intercourse—once an exciting pleasurable expression of love—became little more than the mechanical act of trying to produce a baby.

The process of wondering which partner is responsible for the inability to conceive can cause disharmony and strife in what formerly had been a loving and secure marriage relationship. The situation escalates so that you then have a woman obsessed with only one thing: 'I want a baby!' And you also have a husband who is frustrated and angry because he is doing all he can, and no longer knows how to help or comfort his wife. A man's instinct to be a father is rarely as strong as his wife's maternal instinct.

Situations like this have been going on for thousands of years. In the first book of the Bible are the words:

> When Rachel saw that she was not bearing Jacob any children, she became jealous of her sister. So she said to Jacob, 'Give me children, or I'll die.' Jacob became angry with her and said, 'Am I in the place of God, who has kept you from having children?' (Genesis 30:1).

An obsession

If both wife *and* husband become equally obsessed with having a baby then every part of their lives can be tinged with this shadow—often turning to bitterness and resentment. A situation like that is obviously wrong, for God does not intend his children to live with this kind of emotional cancer, slowly destroying their personalities.

Although Emily's words wounded me and made me angry, God used them to draw my attention to a situation inside myself which was getting out of hand. She made me stop, think and reassess my relationship with Harry. She also made me realize that anyone looking at a bitter and resentful couple was hardly likely to be drawn to the God of Christianity by the quality of their lives.

While we were in Iran the church there recommended that Harry obtain a Bachelor of Divinity degree. So after our return to Scotland Harry enrolled on a two-year Bachelor or Divinity course at Glasgow University. At the end of this time we hoped that the turmoil in Iran would have settled enough for us to return. I filled in some of that time doing a locum in gynaecology but then found myself at a loose end and decided to have a spell as a housewife.

I was not working as a doctor at that point and had too much time on my hands. I found there is nothing worse than moping around the house all day, polishing the coffee table for the third time, and constantly thinking about babies and plaguing myself with questions as to the possible reasons why I didn't have a child.

I decided to try to cope with the anxiety by taking myself in hand, getting a job and going back to work. This helped to fill my days and gave me interest beyond home and my all-consuming inability to conceive. Dealing with other people's problems in my work as a doctor helped me forget my own.

Had I been unable to get work at that time I would have tried one of the many voluntary organizations always glad of help. Alternatively, I could have started some absorbing and creative hobbies. I saw very clearly that I needed *something* to distract me from the draining influence of the wrong kind of anxiety.

False hopes

I realized at that stage that we had fallen into a sort of 'future baby trap'. We were thinking and saying things like: 'We'd better not plan a holiday too far from home this year—I might be pregnant by then.' 'I won't buy a winter coat just yet—if I'm expecting I'll need a loose fitting one.' 'Perhaps I shouldn't apply for promotion in my job—if I conceive then I'll have to leave.' 'I won't apply for that really interesting job I'd love to do as I hope a baby will be on the way before the job starts.'

I had allowed myself to begin to live in a world of '*ifs*'. The future was always obscured by the vague possibility that a baby would figure in it imminently. What I needed more than anything else was to forget about that which was just a possibility, and to deal with present realities. The '*ifs*' of tomorrow would have to take care of themselves. As Jesus said: 'Therefore do not worry about tomorrow, for tomorrow will worry about itself. Each day has enough trouble of its own' (Matthew 6:34). It was good to grasp those words and apply them to myself.

I also realized that there were some situations best avoided at certain times when I knew I would be particularly vulnerable. For example, I did not have to go every week to a certain coffee morning where the conversation was dominated by mums talking non-stop about their children and their latest achievements at school. I found that some of these mums were *totally* absorbed in their children—which is just as bad as me being totally absorbed in trying to have children! Having little in common with such mums I found they were upsetting me and until I felt I could cope it was best to avoid them.

What is God like?

I have found that by far the best antidote to anxiety is a total trust in God, as someone who is good and who loves me. This was an invaluable lesson I was beginning to learn through all that was happening to me. My anxiety had led me to begin to create a mental picture of God's character which had become twisted and distorted. I had started to argue *from* my experience *to* a knowledge of God. I was beginning to think that as God did not give me children he was a Person who was unfeeling and cruel. I needed instead to allow what I know to be true about God's nature to shape my experience—rather than the other way round. I *know* God is good and I *know* God is love. Whether I *feel* this at any given time is not of great importance—of vital importance is the fact that his goodness and love are clearly taught in the Bible.

In other words, I was asking: 'Does my infertility suggest that God no longer loves me? Is it fair of God to deny me children when so many parents mistreat theirs and obviously don't want them? Is God in control of my situation?'

What I needed was to react instead with words like: 'I know that God is good and that he loves me. I've learned this both from the Bible which is true, and from my past experience of his goodness. So, although I can't understand *why* God has denied me children, the fact that he loves me is not altered in any way. I must cling to this fact even when life appears to suggest the contrary. God certainly is in control and he has a plan for my life which will enable things to work out perfectly in the end.'

I had realized that ideas about the nature of love are often confused. I found C. S. Lewis' words helpful:

> . . . By Love most of us mean kindness . . . a senile benevolence whose plan for the universe was simply that it might be truly said at the end of each day, 'a good time was had by all.' . . . There is kindness in Love: but Love and kindness are not coterminous, and when kindness is separated from the other elements of Love, it involves a certain fundamental indifference to its object . . . It is for people whom we care nothing about that we demand happiness on any terms . . . [God] never regarded us with contempt. He has paid us the intolerable compliment of loving us in the deepest, most tragic, most inexorable sense. (*The Problem of Pain*, Geoffrey Bles 1940, Fontana 1957, pp. 28–29.)

The very best

God's love for you and me is far greater than just wanting us to be happy. God desires the very best for each of us. More than that, he wants us to become like Jesus and this process may from time to time involve pain and hurt. I had to learn truly to trust God with my life and believe that he would lead and guide me.

I knew that if I could learn these lessons then overwhelming, paralysing anxiety would be displaced for God would be controlling my life—

rather than my emotions. He would either work things out so that I had children of my own, or he would teach me to live without them and give me the ability to do so without becoming warped or bitter.

I realized that if my happiness and contentment were dependent on the circumstances in which I found myself then I would constantly be disappointed and discontented. Jesus' words brought me great help and comfort: 'I have told you these things, so that *in me* you may have peace. In this world you will have trouble. But take heart! I have overcome the world' (John 16:33).

Source of peace

True and lasting peace lies only in Jesus. Nothing and no one else gives us peace like his. My peace is securely rooted in Jesus himself and in all that he achieved on the cross for me. It helps me to hold on to the fact that Jesus never changes—circumstances change often and Jesus even warns us that life will bring us trouble. Yet, provided our peace and confidence are grounded in him, nothing will shake us from our secure foundation. We can expect our share of life's sorrow and heartbreak—Jesus himself experienced more of this than we ever will—but we will never come adrift if our peace is anchored in Jesus. I am confident that through pain and suffering God is able to change us, increasingly making us more like Jesus Christ—and that is one of God's main purposes for his children.

We are promised in the Bible: 'And we know that in all things God works for the good of those who love him, who have been called according to his purpose. For those God foreknew he also predestined to be conformed to the likeness of his Son' (Romans 8:28–29). I constantly need to remind myself of this for the devil is eager to warp or destroy my peace. If he can get me to focus my attention on something else and cause me to become distracted (distracted to the point of anxiety or even obsession) then my eyes are no longer fixed on Jesus and I land myself in trouble again.

This was what happened to Martha in the New Testament. She thought that their visit from Jesus could only be perfect if she produced a beautiful meal for him. She was so distracted by this that she missed the whole point of the day. The day was perfect already because Jesus was there in her home! That would not change, no matter what the meal was like.

I realized that I too could be oblivious of Jesus' presence in my life if I allowed myself to be distracted by excessive misplaced anxiety. Yes, I must bring my legitimate longing for a baby to God in prayer but I also needed to ask him to protect me from becoming too concerned about it. I needed God to help me do this because I found it nearly impossible by myself.

3

Prayer and Perplexity

Trying to open myself to Emily had produced two results. Yes, I had been hurt, but also I had come to understand myself and God better—so it had been worthwhile in the long run.

I began to feel a need to muster enough courage to attempt sharing my deepest self with someone else. I needed another Christian to help me sort out whether I should simply trust God to give me a child if, and when, he wanted to, or whether God wanted me to take the practical step of going to a clinic for investigation and treatment of infertility.

I remembered another friend who lived near me and felt I knew her well enough to drop in, even though it was her baby's bath time.

Sarah was the picture of motherhood. Unlike me, she had never aimed at establishing a career. Home and family were all she had ever desired. She sailed through her first pregnancy, which started soon after marriage.

I listened as patiently as I could while she talked non-stop about the baby's achievements, his diets, the new wallpaper in the nursery, the self-catering holiday planned in the summer, and so it went on.

On several occasions I tried to broach the subject of my own problem without any success. I had all but given up, when suddenly Sarah said: 'When are you going to start your family?' I seized the opportunity but sensed that she was only half listening while I poured out my longing for a baby.

Pray about it

'Well, the thing to do is to pray about it,' Sarah suggested rather dispassionately. 'Prayer worked for Hannah! It will for you! Leave everything in God's hands.'

Something inside me was squashed by those words. I said no more. I *had* prayed. Sarah had no idea how many hours, days, weeks and months I had spent praying about my longing for a baby. There didn't seem any point in trusting Sarah with any more of my feelings.

Once Sarah had churned out her pat Christian answer—so glibly, simplistically and thoughtlessly—she became totally absorbed in a search for the talcum powder, one specially produced for sensitive skins like her baby's.

I felt even worse after this second attempt at sharing than I had the first time. I had been angry then but now I was near to despair. Sarah seemed so uncaring. Her world revolved around her baby and she appeared oblivious to anything else.

It was no new revelation to me that God had

answered Hannah's prayer for a child. I knew these chapters in the first book of Samuel almost by heart.

In 1 Samuel chapter 1 we are told the moving story of a woman—one of two wives—who longed for, yet remained without, children. Her distress was increased by the agony of having to watch her husband pay attention to his other wife's sons and daughters.

Hannah was greatly distressed and prayed, making a vow to God that if he gave her a child she would 'give him to the Lord for all the days of his life.'

The Lord knew of Hannah's sorrow and was not indifferent to it. He used this situation of great sadness to cradle a child, born to Hannah at exactly the right moment, who was going to be of great significance to the Jewish nation.

The Lord heard Hannah's prayer and Samuel was born.

I had read the story over and over again, along with other parts of the Bible which seemed to promise children. Children seemed to be given as a reward to God's people. Many women written about in the Bible were barren until God answered their prayers and 'opened' their wombs and gave them children. So what was wrong with me? Why didn't God answer my prayers?

Suggesting to an infertile woman that she should pray about her problem is rather redundant. All my infertile Christian friends and acquaintances pray a great deal already about their desire for children. They constantly pray about it.

How should I pray?

For me the question was rather: '*How* should I pray? In what sense might I expect God to answer my prayers? If God says "No" is that an acceptable answer?'

'If God doesn't answer my prayers in the way I assume he should, is it because I don't have enough faith? Is that my problem? Perhaps I don't believe strongly enough?'

'Alternatively, is there something wrong with my Christian life that God is denying me the gift of children?'

Questions like these ran through my mind all the time.

Suggesting to an infertile woman that she should examine Hannah's situation may well just lead to yet more anguish. Some thoughtlessly say that 'it worked for Hannah' as if a simple formula existed for prayer. If you apply it, it will work for you too. They sound as if they believe in prayer as simple cause and effect and that praying would guarantee a baby. This raised deep issues for me. Was I then to approach God as if he was some kind of heavenly vending machine; slip in the right prayer, offered in the right way, pull the right lever and then hold out my arms to catch the baby that would fall into them?

Such thinking results in confusion, increased anguish, and yet more pain. I know—I've been there!

Sarah's words did no more than stir up old feelings of confusion about myself. Was I failing somehow? Was I praying too little or with insufficient faith? Could I expect God to give me anything I wanted as long as it seemed a reasonable request made with enough faith?

By the time I got home from Sarah's, I couldn't do anything other than sit down and sob my heart out. 'Lord, why do I have to go through so much pain?'

God's loving reply

God's gentle and loving reply in response to my tears seemed to be: 'My child, I want to do something remarkable and special in you. I want you to learn through all this hurt and sorrow how to be more like Jesus. I want to draw you nearer to myself.'

Words from the Bible filled my mind with comforting strength and reassurance: '"Though the mountains be shaken and the hills be removed, yet my unfailing love for you will not be shaken nor my covenant of peace be removed," says the Lord, who has compassion on you' (Isaiah 54:10).

> 'For my thoughts are not your thoughts, neither are your ways my ways,' declares the Lord. 'As the heavens are higher than the earth, so are my ways higher than your ways and my thoughts than your thoughts . . . You will go out in joy and be led forth in peace; the mountains and hills will burst into song before you, and all the trees of the field will clap their hands. Instead of the thornbush will grow the pine tree, and instead of briers the myrtle will grow' (Isaiah 55:8–13).

So what did God want me to learn from all that was happening to me? Perhaps I needed to examine these questions systematically. If I could find God's solution then those problems might stop troubling me.

I studied Hannah's story again and pictured the pitfalls into which I had fallen in the past. I read that 'in bitterness of soul Hannah wept much and prayed to the Lord'. I used to reason that possibly God had granted Hannah's request because he saw how distressed she was. He couldn't miss seeing how much she wanted a baby. I began to think that perhaps I didn't make it obvious enough to God that I desperately wanted a baby, so he didn't give me one. I was on dangerous ground! Deep down I knew so well that no amount of distress would 'buy' a baby from God. It would be contrary to God's nature of love to treat me like that. These unhelpful thoughts would bring the almighty Creator God down to my level rather than raising us up to his.

It would never be that the gift of a baby—*always* a free gift of his grace—would be withheld because I hadn't been convincing enough in my display of desperation for that gift.

I realized afresh that God *is* loving and merciful in the way he treats us. God understands me without my screaming my needs out to him. I don't have to impress my needs on him—he knows the depths of my heart.

A false formula

Different people advocate different things about asking God for something specific. Some say: 'When you ask, it must be with "the prayer of faith".' They explain that you must ask and then believe that God has already given you what you requested. You then thank him in advance for what you believe he has already given you.

It seems a simple formula, but does it work? Should prayer work like this?

As I wrestled with the issue of 'praying in faith' I soon began to realize that frequently I fell into the trap of putting faith in my praying rather than in God. It is God who is the object of faith; God who loves me and wants to do me good. The last thing I want to do is to demand things for myself that I am not sure God wants me to have.

Surely we can only have faith to believe that God will give us what we pray for when we are certain that what we are asking for is in line with God's will for us.

It is easy to take Bible words out of context and to draw the wrong conclusions from them—especially verses like: 'My Father will give you whatever you ask in my name' (John 16:23). We may assume that provided we tag on the closing formula 'in Jesus' name' at the end of our prayer we can make and receive our requests. Suppose I want a Rolls Royce. Can I pray 'in Jesus' name' and expect automatically to receive one? You would argue that my having a luxurious car is not God's will for me and that this is a selfish request. It is therefore understandable when the request is refused.

But then surely wanting a baby is a legitimate God-given desire? The Bible shows that God's normal pattern is for a married couple to have children. Should I not pray with faith that God would give a child to me?

As I wallowed in a little self-pity, I suddenly thought of my close university friend still unmarried, yet so much longing for a life partner. It is God's normal pattern for people to get married, and yet some remain single. Similarly, it is not his will for *every* married couple to have children. Therefore, the Bible nowhere says that any couple praying for a child will automatically receive one. There were many things in life I could be quite sure that God would give if I asked in faith—things promised in the Bible like my increased knowledge of himself, my fruitfulness in service, my growth in patience and love—many things—but having a baby was not one of them.

Tactics for failure

Thinking about Hannah I noticed again that she promised to give her child back to God. I wondered: 'Perhaps that's the secret—I need to give God something precious in return for a baby. Maybe if I promise to dedicate the child to God—he can be a missionary or a minister—then God will give me a baby.'

So I promised God that I would bring a child up in exactly the way I thought he would want. The child could leave me and serve God full time if that's what God wanted—anything for a baby!

Of course this tactic was doomed to failure. I had reduced prayer to little more than the level of bribery. Could I make God do what I wanted by trying to bribe him? I realized that this was what I was trying to do. I was saying to God: 'Give me a child and I'll give you someone to serve you.' And God cannot be bargained with like that.

No amount of bargaining can be a key that unlocks God's will. How often I'd thought to myself 'you must be persistent'—remembering Jesus' parable of the persistent widow and also the friend who pestered his friend for bread (Luke 11:5–13). I had to work out whether this really did mean that if we badger God enough and annoy him eventually he will give in to us and grant our requests. Thinking again about my hypothetical desire for a Rolls Royce, there is no way that God would grant such a stupid desire no matter how often or how long I asked for it. To imply that this is possible is to read into these Bible passages what they do not mean to say.

Jesus himself had a request refused by his Father, when in deep distress he recoiled from the cross—knowing it implied bearing the sin of the world and being separated from his Father. In his humanity he prayed three times for the cup to be removed from him if it was possible. But God did not remove the cup; instead God gave Jesus the strength to endure it: 'An angel from heaven appeared to him to strengthen him.' Jesus' request was refused, but his Father *enabled* him to follow a pathway that he had not believed he could endure.

Can we then take Hannah's situation as a sort of broody wife's manual on how to have a baby? Nowhere in Hannah's story does it say that God gave her a child because of anything she had done. It was simply that 'the Lord remembered Hannah and she conceived'. I needed to remind myself that it is because of his love that God gives to me—it is not because of anything I could ever do for him. No matter how perfect I try to be, it will not influence the love God showers on me despite my unworthiness. God will not give me a baby as a reward for being good—it is not as simple as that!

What then can I give God that is not already his? The only thing I can offer him is the access to work freely in and through my life.

God's purposes of grace

Nowhere does the Bible promise children to all who ask. Hannah's experience is *not* for everyone.

But it wasn't just Hannah—there were more barren women who prayed and God gave them a child—Sarah, Rebekah, Rachel, Sampson's mother and Elizabeth. God intervened in all these cases in response to prayer. But I was beginning to see the connecting thread more clearly. In each incident the remarkable thing was that the child conceived played a major role in advancing God's purpose for salvation. The common factor was not that God gives babies to those who ask properly, but rather the amazing way in which God can turn even such a strong traumatic human anguish as childlessness into a means of advancing his purposes of grace. God used each of these difficult situations to cradle the men he planned to use in strategic service. Surely there must have been other women in Israel who prayed for a child but God answered 'no'?

The almighty God cannot be limited to act

according to one set pattern nor is there any magic formula guaranteeing 'success' in prayer. God hears and responds to all prayer but sometimes his answer is 'no' or 'not yet'.

Is there then no purpose in prayer? Will God do what he is going to do regardless of what we are like, and whether we pray urgently, persistently, or with deep emotional pain? The Bible urges us to pray and it is amazing to realize that God graciously condescends to work through our prayers and that the Scriptures encourage us to come to him with our petitions.

Prayer is communion

I was learning that prayer is much more than simply bringing our deepest needs to God. It is primarily *communion* with God himself. It is not a heavenly mail order service—though many treat it like this and only pray when they want something. This was a danger I had to learn to avoid. Were my prayers becoming baby-centred rather than God-centred? Was it only when I wanted a baby so badly that I was driven to prayer as a last resort? If I was doing that then I had missed the point of prayer—of coming to a loving Father and bringing to him all that is in my heart, seeking understanding of his will, his help and his answer.

I had to study and think a lot before I could understand the part prayer should play in my painful situation. My friend, Sarah, had told me to 'pray about it'. She had failed to tell me *how* to pray and I had learned that prayer was far more than me trying to persuade God to give me what I wanted. I learned that another aspect of prayer, as communion with a God with whom I could build a close relationship, was bringing hurt feelings quickly to him so that they would not fester and erupt into bitterness and resentment. I learned that God cared about my feelings, he loved me and wanted me to open my heart to him.

I also learned that all too often I was praying for the wrong things. I needed to understand that when God seemed to be saying 'no' I should learn to accept this instead of trying to bribe him and twist his arm (as if I really could!)

I needed to reach the place of praying: 'Lord you know my heart's desire. If you are saying "no" or "not yet" then help me cope with that. Help me to learn what you want to teach me from this. Give me grace to accept your will especially when I don't understand it. Show me how I can have a rich and fulfilling life without children. Please help . . . for I am asking a great deal and I do need your help.'

Accepting God's will

Something was happening to me through all this. Now I was learning increasingly to submit to Jesus' lordship of my life. And with submission to God's will for me, acceptance of my situation was growing. Instead of a determined 'I want my desires fulfilled' I was learning to say and to mean 'Your will not mine'. When Jesus prayed in the garden of Gethsemane he asked for 'the cup' to be removed but added 'Your will not mine' (Luke 22:41–43). I was learning to develop this attitude and the process of my becoming more like Jesus was continuing.

Some Christians think that they are helping by encouraging infertile couples to keep on praying. 'Don't give up, persist in praying for a baby for then surely God will give you one.' It is not necessarily wrong to go on praying for a child, but it is wrong to encourage others into false optimism which can lead to shattered hopes and disillusionment. A Christian has to learn to be willing to accept whatever answer God gives.

Submission to God and acceptance of his will are vital keys in coping with childlessness. They give God a free hand to fashion us and turn us into the people he wants us to be. Archbishop Robert Leighton once said, 'Adversity is the diamond dust heaven polishes its jewels with.' (Tony Castle, *The Hodder Book of Christian Quotations*, Hodder and Stoughton 1982, p.5.)

This understanding was a major turning point for me. I was able to put my hand in God's and say: 'Yes Lord, I *do* trust you. I trust you with my life and your plans for me.' And then God began to enrich life in many different ways despite my childlessness. Where I was empty I trusted God to fill the void. That was my 'prayer of faith' and God did so much for me.

Whether God gives the childless babies or not, he never fails to supply grace to his children to cope with difficulties in their lives. He always answers our prayers when we are helpless and cannot carry the burden of pain alone. If we allow him to, he will use crucibles of suffering to refine us and make us more like Jesus. When Jesus submitted to his Father's will, God gave him the strength he needed to endure what lay ahead. When we submit to God's loving purposes for us, then he will enable us to go through anything that may be painful.

Be totally frank

Sometimes we must be totally frank and ask ourselves: 'Do I want to wallow in self-pity, miserable that God has denied me what he has given others? Or do I really want to see what God can and will do in and for me. Do I honestly want his help or not?'

Hudson Taylor—a great missionary pioneer—wrote after one particularly painful emotional experience:

> We have need of patience, and our faithful God brings us into experiences which, improved by His blessing, may cultivate in us this grace. Though we seemed to be tried at times beyond endurance, we never find Him unable or unwilling to help and sustain us. And were our hearts entirely submissive to His will, desiring it and it only to be done, how much fewer and lighter would our afflictions seem to be. I have had much sorrow of late, but the cause I find to be want of willing submission to and trustful repose in God, my strength. Oh to desire His will to be done with my whole heart and to seek His glory with a single eye.

But, having learned one lesson, I next had to discover the pitfall of confusing submission to God's will for me with fatalism and passiveness—doing nothing because 'if God wants me to have a baby he'll make it happen'.

I have found that another response to prayer is that from time to time God uses my prayers to encourage me to take practical action myself, and in this case to think through the possibility of going for investigation and treatment of infertility. It could be that God's answer to my prayers was neither 'no' nor 'not yet' but rather: 'Go and get something done about it yourself.' That meant facing doctors and clinics and tests. I wasn't sure about that yet.

4
Fear and Guidance

You might assume that because I am a doctor it would seem sensible and logical to me to go to a 'sub-fertility clinic' for investigation and possible treatment for my childlessness. After all, when I have a pain somewhere I go to the doctor, and may then be referred to hospital for tests and X-rays which will show what is wrong with me. Then, if it is treatable, I usually go ahead with whatever the specialists recommend should be done.

I felt, however, that infertility came into a different category from other kinds of medical problems. Surely, I reasoned, as a Christian I ought to be able to trust God completely in this whole area? After all, he is the Creator of all life and his power is so great that he could perform a miracle of healing in me and give me a baby (if a miracle was going to be the answer in my case).

These two threads of thought were like a tug of war going on in my mind. On the one hand I believed in God both as the author of life and as the worker of miracles, able to give life within me if he wanted to. On the other hand my intellect and reason assured me that medical treatment was a sensible and logical course of action to take.

Paralysing fear

Eventually careful thought and analysis of my conflicting feelings about going to an infertility clinic uncovered the fact that the root cause of my indecision was fear, and not lack of belief in God's omnipotence.

I have discovered that fear is a dark blanket which the devil uses to blind and confuse Christians. It paralyses many of us causing us to be indecisive and inactive. Whatever its cause, the result all too often is to shroud us from God and his love so that we remain trapped in a circle of numbing fear. And God does not intend us to be like this as the Bible explains: 'God is love . . . there is no fear in love. But perfect love drives out fear, because fear has to do with punishment. The man who fears is not made perfect in love' (1 John 4:16–18).

Fear can have devastating effects on us as Christians. It can so stunt our growth as Christians that we are afraid to move out in any direction and end up standing still or even sliding backwards away from God. The sad fact is that many of us are not aware of our deep-seated fear and the confusion it causes us.

God was loving and patient in gradually revealing to me the fears in my heart and the way he wanted me to deal with them. Even when I thought some were behind me, they would flicker to flame again and throw me back into confusion.

As I have shared with other infertile women I have discovered that my fears were common to most of them, whether they recognized it or not. Unfortunately many women are paralysed by these fears for so long that when they finally take action, they are in their thirties and have a reduced number of years in which it might be possible for them to have a baby.

Fear of the unknown

The first fear I uncovered was fear of the unknown. Many childless women glean snippets of information—some true and some false—which produce an unspecified feeling of gloom. This can distort their thinking and attitudes and influence decision-making or lack of it.

As a doctor I had never worked in an infertility clinic myself and so was not sure of the exact procedures that were routinely followed. I had done some gynaecology and so I knew to a limited extent what would be involved. But a little knowledge can be worse than none. I hated the idea of being a patient myself and perhaps being admitted to a ward. My imagination worked overtime and fear was having a paralysing effect on me.

I know some Christians who have been married for years without conceiving a baby. Although the pain and anguish of this has been almost unbearable, they have not attempted to discover any God-given options and alternatives to remaining childless. They have been like ostriches burying their heads in the sand, and hoping that if they ignore their situation the problems will disappear. They feel the only acceptable alternative is for God to work a miracle for them—that way they face no trauma or fuss or bother.

However, those of us who are childless, through no choice of our own, have to face our situations and deal with our fears of the unknown by finding out what is involved if we are going to break a link in the chain of our crippling indecision.

Fear of others

The next fear which I admitted with reluctance, was the fear of what other people would think of me. I imagined pitying voices saying: 'She can't have children you know. What a shame.' 'Pity Ray can't have a baby, isn't it?' Or accusing voices: 'Fancy Ray going to an infertility clinic. You'd think someone like her would have more trust in God than to do a thing like that.'

I had to ask myself why I was so taken up with what other people might think of me. I don't like to think of people pitying me or thinking wrong of me, but what does it really matter provided I am convinced that I am doing what God wants me to do? Many of us tend often to be more concerned about having man's approval than God's. When we fall into this trap as Christians, then we have got our priorities wrong. Concern that we are obeying God must be our prime concern.

Pride is also a major factor. We don't want to admit openly that we have any weaknesses. We want others to think well of us, and to say complimentary things like: 'What a mature Christian she is.'

It is of course wrong for us to go around exposing and revealing the depths of our heart to a lot of people as not everyone will understand. Yet I believe we Christians should be more open and honest with each other—admitting some of our failures and weaknesses, and not being shocked by anything others share with us. It is easy to wear a mask and to parade a good public image which conceals an underlying mass of fear and insecurity.

Our decisions must not be totally determined by the opinions of other Christians. While it *is* good and helpful to seek the advice of mature Christian friends, ultimately we are responsible ourselves for seeking and understanding God's will for our lives and for going ahead with what we believe to be his plan for us. We are answerable to God for the decisions we make and the actions we take.

Infertility is so personal that I have found it hard to share my deepest feelings about it with any except a few close friends (often those who share a similar problem) and with my husband. This is partly the result of having been hurt by people who are not gifted with the sensitivity or imagination to begin to understand the depths of disappointment and pain of infertile couples.

It doesn't make much difference what people say to the contrary, many of us still feel there is some stigma attached to being infertile. Even the Bible suggests this. Rachel, after Joseph's birth said: 'God has taken away my disgrace' (Genesis

30:23). And Elizabeth, when she knew she was pregant, said: 'The Lord has done this for me. In these days he has shown his favour and taken away my disgrace among the people' (Luke 1:25). Infertile men and women have a deep sense of failure. They are not able to function as others can.

The Christian, however, is not left alone with these feelings. We can bring all these fears to God in prayer and ask him to help us deal with them. Constantly reminding myself and meditating on the fact that God knows and understands all my feelings has helped me greatly. When other people fail to understand us or even misunderstand us, the all-understanding God is there. He knows the contents of our hearts and he lovingly cares about us.

Because God became man, he knows how we feel in our human hurts and suffering. Jesus was more misunderstood, pitied, despised, and rejected than we will ever be. I find it helpful to remind myself of this comforting and strengthening fact.

Fear of disobeying God

The next fear which stopped me from making an appointment at the sub-fertility clinic was a fear that I might be doing something God did not want me to do, and of going out of line with God's will for me. This is a real fear for many Christians who take their discipleship seriously and it may paralyse them so that in the end they do nothing. So afraid are they of taking a wrong step, that fear rules their lives making them afraid to change jobs, move house, choose a marriage partner or get involved in Christian work and so on. They feel safer to stay exactly where they are. 'Don't rock the boat or change the status quo!' is their unconscious unspoken motto.

Christians rarely recognize this when it is the true underlying reason for inactivity. Some assume they are 'very spiritual' and remark: 'I must wait until God tells me to do it!' or 'I don't *feel* led to do that.'

Such Christians generally have a very shaky foundation on which they have constructed their thinking about how God guides his children. Their doctrine of guidance is built on feelings and emotions. This leads to confusion and disappointment. Many want God to give them a 'special Bible verse' on which to base their actions, and others will not be convinced until they see something as dramatic as God's directions written in gold letters in the sky.

I had to learn these lessons about my fears before I could apply them to my own situation. I had to think through how God could and would guide me about the rights and wrongs of going for investigations and possible treatment, rather than allow myself to be paralysed by fear of doing something that would put me outside God's will for my life.

God began to teach me clearly that not only did he want to guide me about my infertility but also that he had promised to do this. One verse (out of many) in the Bible that helped me was God's reassurance: 'I will instruct you and teach you in the way you should go; I will counsel you and watch over you' (Psalm 32:8).

Many Christians have a warped idea of how God guides his children. We assume everything depends on us coming to the right decision by ourselves, and God stands peeping behind the curtains of heaven biting his nails, waiting to see if we make the decision he wants us to or not. Then he shouts 'Hurrah!' if we get it right and 'Too bad!' if we don't. Such concepts turn guidance into a virtual game of chance. We would be right to be afraid of decision-making if such were the factors that governed the possibility of staying in God's will.

Am I willing to obey?

If we genuinely seek God's will then he won't hide it from us. I believe that some of the difficulties we have in understanding God's will are often ones we manufacture ourselves. We bring in complication after complication because of our needless fears. Sometimes our real problem lies more in the realm of our being willing to obey God rather than of his 'unwillingness' to guide us. He cannot reveal to us what he wants us to do until we are ready to act in obedience to him. We cannot say to God: 'Tell me what you want, and then I'll decide whether I want to obey or not.' Until we are ready to obey, God often does not reveal his will for us in a particular situation.

God would not be a God of love if he were to allow those of his children who sincerely desire to follow his will to wander down wrong paths which end in disaster. Because of our complex thinking patterns, we may take a wrong turning from time to time, but as we constantly bring our situation to him, honestly seeking his perfect plan for our lives, he makes sure we do not go in the wrong direction for too long. Sometimes he uses this to guide us onto the right path. He loves us and wants us to discern his will for us. He never makes it unnecessarily complicated.

How does God guide us?

God's most important method of communicating with us is through the Bible. In this book he has revealed much of his character, and given some basic principles which should govern our lives.

When I was a new Christian and wanted to know God's guidance, I used to open my Bible at random and place my finger on the first verse it came to. If this could be applied to my particular situation then I used it to do so. If it could not, then I repeated the process until my finger landed on a verse which suited me. I am surprised to find that many other Christians use this sort of lucky dip method in seeking God's guidance—and it is not only new Christians who do so! My experience is that such a method ends only in confusion and even disaster, apart from very rare exceptions!

Understanding God's will does not depend on such a game of chance. Rather it depends on Christians studying and grasping the broad principles for living taught in Scripture and applying them to daily life and differing situations.

Medical help or miracles?

What broad principles can those of us who are childless take from the Bible to help us discover whether it is right to seek medical help or not?

Jesus healed people who were ill during his ministry on earth, and God miraculously intervened to give children to certain barren women in the Old Testament. Some would infer from these two facts that unless God intervenes miraculously an infertile couple have no other options open to them. However, this is misusing the Bible to make it appear that the spectacular and miraculous is the rule—rather than a special example of God's providential care for us—of love given in an unusual way.

Consider the way God provides food for us to eat. It is true that God caused the ravens to operate a 'meals on wings' service to feed the prophet Elijah at the brook Kerith (1 Kings 17:3–4). It is also true that the children of Israel were pursued through the desert by God's fast food service (Exodus 16). But neither of these were God's usual way of providing food for his children. God encouraged his people to use all the ordinary means of provision that they could. They were not to expect miracles to be God's normal way of helping them.

When we pray 'give us this day our daily bread' we do not limit God by expecting him to act in a spectacular way with an angel arriving on our doorstep each morning with a loaf of bread from the heavenly bakery. We accept that our work earns the money necessary for us to buy our material provisions. And this in itself is part of God's providential and fatherly care for us.

Once we move into the realm of healing I believe that similarly God does not want us to limit his help to the miraculous and spectacular. God does sometimes graciously and mercifully intervene to heal by miraculous means, but his norm for us is through the medical profession, and the understanding of illness given to them by God.

Why is it that some find it easy to accept medical help for a heart condition or arthritis, but they insist that the infertile must trust God to heal miraculously or not at all? Can we not seek medical help and still trust God to heal? Some of us need to accept the way God normally provides for us before we expect anything out of the ordinary. This acceptance by an infertile couple may involve getting medical help.

The turning point in my thinking occurred one day when my husband asked me: 'If you had anything else wrong and needed a doctor you wouldn't hesitate. Why is it different when something may be wrong with your reproductive system?'

Thanks be for male logic! Of course logic won over emotions! And when I studied biblical principals, I could find no valid reason for not attending the infertility clinic.

Circumstantial guidance

Our particular circumstances must never be used as the only criteria on which we base our guidance, but God *may* use circumstances to help us see the options open to us. For instance, your nearest infertility clinic may be miles away involving time and expense for each visit and this may make you feel you should limit medical help to your own GP and the local hospital. Or you may already have a medical problem which would be made worse by investigations or treatment for infertility, and even worse by a pregnancy. You may feel that this situation is an important part of God guiding you to accept things as they are without seeking further medical help.

However, if there is no good reason why you could not or should not attend an infertility clinic, and you long to try to have a baby, then I think you would need God's clear guidance *not* to get help.

God also guides us through unspectacular sanctified common sense. We have to think things out rather than act on our feelings. Sanctified reason and logic are God-given means for working out a decision. In the past my fragile feelings and see-saw emotions have often tied me up in knots over decision-making. When I think calmly and sensibly I make decisions much better!

The last hurdle of fear I had to overcome was fear about the personal cost of having infertility investigations. It would have been easier and preferable to me had God granted my prayer request effortlessly and without any fuss. I knew he could do that. Why didn't he? Most women get pregnant effortlessly so why did I have to suffer the humiliation of attending an infertility clinic? Why did I have to go through tests and treatments? I wanted a 'simple miracle'. But God had other plans for me.

I dreaded visits to hospitals where I might bump into friends and colleagues, and have to explain what I was doing there. I preferred them not to know about my personal sadness. I did not want to go through embarrassing investigations and possible treatment later on that might be painful or require great commitment in terms of time and effort. There would also be the inevitable disappointments and, in the end, perhaps no baby to make it all worth while.

I considered the alternatives. These fears could be allowed to imprison me. I could refuse to try to find out the cause of our infertility but if I did this I might have to live with the nagging regret of having done nothing while time was on our side. I might always wonder if I had turned my back on the possibility of medical attention which would have enabled us to have children.

Conquering fear

Alternatively I could face my fears and try to conquer them. This did not imply that I would definitely go for investigations but it would enable me to make a rational decision, based on that which I believed was God's will for me. I would not then live with a sense of regret.

Although I finally decided to attend the infertility clinic, some of my basic fears did remain—mainly those of not wanting anyone to know that I was going to such a clinic. I found it difficult to share my pent-up unfulfilled desires with others. So I did not chat to any who had already been investigated. Perhaps this wasn't necessary for me as my medical background gave me insights into what would happen, but I think it could have been a help to receive encouragement and moral support from others. If you are thinking of embarking on the infertility investigation trail then do try to find someone who has been through it and chat it all over with them first. Forewarned is forearmed. A few simple questions at this stage could quickly show that any fear you had of investigations had been fuelled unjustifiably by a vivid imagination.

Togetherness is vital

By far the most important help I found in all of this was my husband's support. I do think it is vitally important that everything is talked through together, and that both partners agree on a course of action. A joint decision is necessary even though only one partner may require treatment. Treatment can be an arduous process which demands time and commitment and the one who is being treated will cope much better if he or she is sure of continuous loving encouragement and support from the other.

If the decision is made against having investigations done, it is still every bit as important that both partners are agreed on this. If not, then there is real danger that at some future date, resentment may gain a foothold in the heart of either the husband or wife who really wanted the investigations carried out. Resentment can undermine even the most stable of marriages.

As we come to our decision, we need to recognize that we are all different. What may be good and right for one couple, may not be for another. Therefore, it is quite unacceptable to argue: 'Because one couple decide it is not right for them to be investigated, it cannot be right for anyone.'

A personal decision

Harry and I talked long and hard on many occasions about the pros and cons of our personal situation. Every couple has to work out their own response to the idea of going ahead with investigations and it should be an active process, coming to a firm decision one way or the other, rather than a shelving of the issue in the hope that investigations may not be necessary. Some couples continually refuse to sit down and talk through their problems. Every time the suggestion to have investigations and treatment comes into their heads, they dismiss it saying: 'We'll think about it later.' It is only reasonable to say that you must set a firm deadline for a decision to be made, otherwise you will never have peace about the matter.

It can take a considerable time for investigations to be completed and treatment instigated. At the end of the day, you may still not be able to have children of your own and at this juncture, you may wish to consider adoption. If you have left it too long, you may find that you have passed the age limit for adopting. It is sensible, therefore, that a couple at least carefully consider all the possibilities as soon as they think they may be infertile.

Some of the questions which Harry and I had to ask were: 'Could we cope with the continuing uncertainty of wondering if there was something wrong which could be easily rectified? Could we cope with remaining childless? Some couples find this easier than others. They may be fully satisfied in their careers and other avenues. Other couples may clearly see God's purpose in their childlessness and be willing to accept it in order to serve God in a particular way. But what of us? We began to sense that in our case it would be wrong not to at least embark on the path of seeking medical advice.

You must make the appropriate decision for you and stick to it, but first, ask yourself the question: 'When I am forty years old and still have no children, will I regret not at least finding out what was wrong? What if it was something simple which could have been corrected?'

5

Testing Times

It was a long three months' wait for my first appointment at the infertility clinic. Then at last I was sitting in the waiting room with my husband. I remember so well the familiar hospital smell in my nose and the small table littered with outdated magazines to wile away seemingly endless time. I was relieved that all the faces around me were anonymous and hoped that no one whom we knew would come in. Each face looked as tense and anxious as we felt.

At last our names were called and we went in to see both a urologist and a gynaecologist. After a brief interview we separated. Harry stayed with the urologist while I followed the gynaecologist into his consulting room.

Should you decide to have infertility investigations, by far the best place to go is a genuine 'sub-fertility' clinic. It is usually called a 'sub-fertility' clinic because no one is classified as 'infertile' until they have been *proved* to be so.

Going to a clinic

These clinics are geared to specialize in the problem of childlessness. Many gynaecologists admit that infertility is so complex and involves such complicated programmes of treatment, that it requires greater knowledge than they have—unless they themselves have specialized in this field. Not many specialize in infertility and therefore 'subfertility' clinics are few and far between—which accounts for long waiting lists for appointments. Such is the demand on limited resources that the waiting time can now be six months or more for a first appointment.

For some the waiting time can be frustrating and the process of attending a sub-fertility clinic stressful. On the other hand, many other couples are so relieved that at last something is actually being done to try to help them that much of the stress they felt earlier is removed.

I fell into the former category finding the whole experience difficult and my patience greatly tested. However, I have no regrets about going. I know that in the long run I would have found it even more difficult living with the uncertainty of not knowing what (if anything) was wrong with me or Harry.

The causes of infertility are complicated and are not yet *fully* understood—I doubt if they ever will be! Doctors often have to admit that they don't know why a particular couple has no children. Encouragingly, much research has been carried out in recent years, and considerable advances both in diagnosis and treatment have been made.

Making the diagnosis

The first problem facing my specialist was that of coming to a correct diagnosis. Without a clear understanding of the cause of infertility in each couple, treatment will be carried out in the dark, and could prove a waste of time, effort and resources.

Our preliminary investigations were designed to pinpoint the particular problems leading to our apparent infertility. Factors affecting fertility are broken down into three different broad areas. Once the problem is identified as coming from one of these areas, detailed investigations can be carried out as necessary. The areas are infertility on the part of the man; some abnormality (either from birth or because of disease) in the structure of any part of the woman's reproductive system; and the abnormal functioning of the woman's reproductive system.

When we finally received our appointment it was for both Harry and me. It is important that both husband and wife are seen and investigated at the clinic. There is little point in investigating one partner only. Should some abnormality be discovered and corrected in one partner this does not rule out the possibility of the other *also* having something wrong.

In fact sub-fertility clinics usually insist on the willingness of both partners to be investigated before they proceed with further investigations. Minor problems are often detected in both partners, and it is the combined effects of these which reduces their fertility as a couple.

Male fertility

Male fertility is affected by factors causing both the production and the ejaculation of sperm. Harry was given a general medical examination by a urologist, and his semen was examined to make sure that his sperm count was adequate both in terms of quantity and quality. Sperm counts vary from time to time and often an initial examination reported as 'inadequate' is followed by one some weeks later which is totally adequate and normal. This is the reason why a second specimen should always be examined if the first appears unsatisfactory.

Although sympathy for infertility is usually given more to the wife, it must be realized that some men also feel deeply about the whole issue. A man is likely to feel inadequate if tests register a low sperm count or even a complete absence of sperms. He may feel that his 'manhood' is threatened and the news may come as a blow making him feel he is not adequate sexually—despite the fact that the level of the sperm count does not affect a man's ability to make love to his wife, nor does it diminish his masculinity in any way. It is the same whether his sperm count is high or low.

Low or absent sperm counts in men arise from different causes. Mumps in childhood or adult life can affect the testes so that they produce no, or very few, sperms. If there has been any problem with testes which have not descended into the scrotal sacs or have descended late in childhood then a low sperm count may result. A varicocele (a varicose vein) on the testes can also impair sperm production. A few medicines have been found to affect the sperm count adversely. Any long serious illness can do likewise.

While it is true that only one sperm is required to fertilize an egg it appears that in order for that one sperm to do its work of fertilization it requires the company of thousands more. In fact, the lower limit of a normal sperm count is 20,000,000 sperms in one millilitre of fluid. While this is a great deal, anything less will reduce the chances of conception. Even if the number of sperms is adequate the chances of pregnancy are reduced if many of them are abnormal or swim very slowly.

When Harry heard that his sperm count was 'normal' he was very relieved. He had found the whole procedure to be embarrassing and stressful. He readily admitted that he would have found it difficult had he required further hospital visits and investigation.

I really appreciated his willingness to have this particular test as many men refuse, insisting that the problem must lie with the wife and that she should be investigated on her own.

Female fertility

When I first saw the gynaecologist I had a routine examination to make sure the pelvic part of my reproductive system was normal. I was told that more investigations might be necessary later to check the ovaries and fallopian tubes. Blood samples were taken to measure certain hormone levels to see if they were normal or not. An assessment of my general fitness was also made so that the gynaecologist could know whether there was any health problem that could influence my fertility.

Two major factors affect female fertility. Either something prevents sperms from reaching the egg, or no egg is available to be fertilized. Investigations of the woman are designed to find out which, if any, problems exist.

A sperm can fail in its attempt to swim up the neck of the womb (the cervical canal) because of something called 'cervical hostility'. This occurs when the mucus produced by a wife's cervix poisons the husband's sperms and kills them.

To see whether this is happening or not a sample of mucus is obtained in the same way that a cervical smear is carried out. A little mucus is placed on one end of a microscope slide and the husband's sperms are put on the other end of the slide. Under the microscope the sperms are then brought into contact with the cervical mucus. Normally sperms are unaffected by contact with mucus. If they stop moving on contact with the mucus, it means that they have been killed and the state of 'cervical hostility' exists between the wife's mucus and the husband's sperms.

The next possible problem that needs investigating is whether sperms can get along the fallopian tubes and reach the eggs or not. Usually an egg is fertilized in one of the fallopian tubes, and it then travels down the tube into the uterus where hopefully it will be implanted in the wall of the uterus.

Tubal blockage

Obviously, if the tubes are blocked, eggs and sperms cannot meet. There are a number of different causes of damage to the tubes—like previous infection or surgery that may lead to scarring and blocking.

Three tests are available to see whether the tubes are open or not. The one which is known as 'utero-tubal insufflation' is less accurate than the others but it is simple and is often carried out if a D & C is being performed. Air is blown into the uterus through a tube connected to a graph meter. If the air flows through the uterus and on up the tubes a normal reading is obtained on the graph paper. If the air cannot get through the tubes, the reading is higher due to an increased pressure in the womb.

Another, more useful, test is a hystero-salpingogram. A tiny tube of dye is inserted up the neck of the womb. Then X-rays are taken showing where the dye travels, and whether the fallopian tubes are open or closed. The X-ray also gives a good outline of the interior of the uterus. Any uterine abnormalities which might hinder the implantation of a fertilized egg or cause frequent miscarriages can sometimes be detected by this method. This procedure is uncomfortable and sometimes even a little painful but it is simple and accurate and carries practically no risk. It can be carried out without a general anaesthetic.

The third method—laparoscopy—is more comprehensive and usually is only carried out when absolutely necessary and when other tests have not already revealed the cause of the problem. Two small incisions are made, one just below the umbilicus and the other about three inches lower down. Air is then blown into the abdominal cavity through one incision, and a viewing instrument like a telescope on the end of a tube is put into the other incision. The air blows out the abdominal wall so that all the pelvic area can easily be seen and any abnormalities detected. Dye is then inserted into the uterus, and can be seen by the instrument, as it comes out of the fallopian tubes into the abdominal cavity. If the tubes are blocked the dye cannot be seen.

This useful investigation gives doctors a clear view of ovaries, uterus, fallopian tubes and the whole pelvic area. Major surgery is unnecessary. However, the laparoscopy involves a general anaesthetic, making this slightly less risk-free than the earlier two tests. It is relatively simple and widely used. A few days' stay in hospital is necessary to recover completely from it.

Problems with ovulation

Other investigations are geared to determine whether the menstrual cycle is normal and whether ovulation is occurring each month or not.

Ovulation (the release of eggs from the ovary every month) is controlled by certain hormones produced by the ovaries and the pituitary gland. The ovaries and the pituitary gland are in different parts of the body but their functioning is connected, and abnormality in one affects the other.

Menstruation (the cyclical shedding of the lining of the uterus) can usually be considered as a sign that conception and implantation of a fertilized egg has not occurred. The cycle usually lasts twenty-eight to thirty days. Day one is reckoned as the first day of four to five days of bleeding. The cycle is divided into two parts by ovulation. This normally occurs fourteen days before the bleeding phase which marks the end of one cycle and the beginning of the next.

The first half of the cycle (before ovulation) is called the 'proliferative phase' when the uterus is preparing for possible implantation of a fertilized egg. The 'luteal' or 'secretory phase' occurs after ovulation and goes on until the end of the cycle. The lining of the womb continues to get ready for pregnancy to occur but once a drop in hormone levels (particularly progesterone) indicates that pregnancy has not taken place, the lining shrinks ready to be shed.

During the cycle, the ovaries (which are full of eggs from before birth) are quite active. Under the influence of hormones one of the eggs matures and ripens. When it reaches the correct size it is released from the ovary ready to be caught by the end of the fallopian tube. The egg then travels down the tube hoping to meet a sperm to fertilize it.

Anything which interferes with this cycle can be a cause of infertility.

The first line of attack in seeing whether the menstrual cycle is normal or not, is to check hormone levels in blood samples to see whether they are present in correct quantities at different times in the cycle.

Then the patient may be asked to record her temperature on a chart throughout her menstrual cycle since this usually indicates whether ovulation is occurring or not.

I well remember my two months given over to this procedure—the wearing business of recording my temperature (basal body temperature) first thing every morning as soon as I awoke. As I charted my temperature every day, I was looking for the emergence of a clear pattern. If ovulation occurs there is a sudden drop followed by a rise in temperature at the time of ovulation. It was actually a relief to me when the two months were over as I sensed how easily I could become preoccupied with my temperature variation.

If doubt still exists as to whether ovulation is taking place or not, a D & C may be performed. In the second part of the cycle (the luteal phase) if ovulation has occurred the lining of the uterus has a characteristic appearance under a microscope.

Ultrasound

At some infertility centres a much more accurate technique is now being employed. This involves using ultrasound investigations combined with examination of daily blood samples. By the use of ultrasound, the doctor can actually watch the egg growing in the ovary and can check that it is growing properly and to the size required for ovulation to take place. The growing egg can be traced up to and just after ovulation. Matching these ultrasound pictures with blood hormone levels reveals accurately and in depth what is happening in the menstrual cycle.

This technique is time consuming both for doctor and patient. But when available it is extremely helpful, accurate and without risk.

It is amazing what the medical profession can now do to come to a correct diagnosis of causes of infertility. I was wrongly diagnosed at first because at that time investigations were less well developed and I was given the wrong type of treatment which could never have helped me. Later, after further investigations, I was diagnosed correctly and put on the correct treatment.

The conclusion of the initial tests I had, showed that I was not ovulating properly, probably due to an abnormality in my pituitary gland. I had a high blood level of a hormone called 'prolactin' which often is associated with a tiny benign tumour in the pituitary gland. The doctors tried some treatment with medicines but disappointingly it did not work.

At this point we were ready to return to missionary work overseas. Harry had completed his Bachelor of Divinity degree, but the situation in Iran had not improved enough for our return there and so our missionary society asked us to consider going out to Pakistan.

After much prayer and thought we believed that this was indeed the next step which God wanted us to take. There was one problem—I would not be able to continue my infertility treatment. I spoke to my gynaecologist who agreed that I could take a six-month supply of my current medication with me to Pakistan.

To many it would seem strange to go to Pakistan and abandon expert medical help in infertility thus jeopardizing our hopes of having a child of our own. However, when we first embarked upon infertility investigations we knew that our intention was to return to Iran when Harry had finished his B.D. Therefore we knew that it would only be for a limited period of time. We had prayed much about seeking help for our childlessness in the first place and had committed our whole lives to God, including our desires for a family. We believed it would have been wrong to refuse to go to Pakistan just so that I could continue with treatment here. Actually when we got to Pakistan we discovered an English gynaecologist who was well qualified and willing to help me continue with my infertility treatment if I wanted to.

Not long after our arrival in Pakistan I contracted amoebic dysentry and became quite ill with it. Eventually we were advised to return home to Scotland for medical treatment. We were also advised not to return to Pakistan—it seemed that I could not cope physically with the health hazards of that country.

God then led Harry into the Church of Scotland ministry. It took me quite some time to regain my physical strength and then I started doing some part-time work in general practice. During that time I returned to the infertility clinic and because quite some time had elapsed since I had last been there it was felt that I should have some further investigations.

After these investigations using the ultrasound combined with blood samples method, a correct diagnosis was made that my menstrual cycle was abnormal. I had what is called 'premature leutinization'. This occurs if the pituitary and ovary link is somehow upset. The second half of each of my cycles was being triggered off early. This meant that each month the follicle in my ovary was getting too little time to ripen and develop adequately. In effect this prevented normal ovulation taking place.

The time factor

Making the correct diagnosis does not automatically mean that successful pregnancy is guaranteed. But there is certainly more likelihood of it if you are on the right treatment!

Investigations may take time. A cycle which lasts a whole month (for some women longer) has to be studied. Some investigations take place over *several* cycles, and time soon mounts up. And because the available facilities are overstretched, there may be waiting lists for certain investigations. This is at least one good reason for thinking about investigations sooner rather than later.

6

Cause and Effect

Couples proceeding along the trail of investigations of the cause of their infertility eventually discover that they fall into one of four categories.

There may be a fertility problem due to the husband; there may be one due to the wife; the problem may arise from something in both husband and wife; or no medical problem may be picked up that accounts for their childlessness.

Without thinking much about it, you might assume that the best category in which to find yourself would be the fourth one where no medical problem is diagnosed. No abnormality is detected after all investigations have been completed. However, such a couple is still left with the uncomfortable question: 'But why haven't we conceived yet? We've been trying long enough.' They are left with a sense of uncertainty—each wondering: 'Am I infertile or am I not? The doctors say there's nothing wrong, but that doesn't explain why we do not have a baby. . . .'

As already stated, infertility is complex and all the factors leading to it have not yet fully been identified or understood. It is therefore possible that some couples within this fourth group are suffering from a cause of infertility which doctors cannot yet pinpoint due to insufficient knowledge. And specific treatment can be given only when the diagnosis is clear. Nowadays many couples in this category are offered in-vitro fertilization (IVF).

But supposing you feel that IVF is not an acceptable option on ethical or on other grounds (see chapter 8)? Then what alternatives are there? How do you cope with your situation?

But the fact that no abnormality is detected and therefore no treatment is prescribed comes as a great relief to many such couples. They are reassured, and this can be a trigger which releases tension, allowing them to begin to relax. When this happens, and stress is relieved, pregnancy may follow. On the other hand tension is increased for other couples. They feel they must try harder. As months and even years pass and conception fails to occur their stress increases even more. Some begin to feel: 'Surely this clinic has missed something—there *must* be *something* wrong.'

Counselling needs

As I have chatted to couples who fall into this category I have seen that the hardest thing they have to cope with is the uncertainty. Many are dejected and feel let down. They went to the clinic to get help, and as far as they were concerned they received none. They went to find out what needed doing so that they could have a baby, and they were told that nothing was wrong; that there was no reason why pregnancy did not occur.

Such couples need counselling by experienced people—but unfortunately this is rarely available at sub-fertility clinics. Counselling consumes time, and this is a precious commodity in such busy clinics.

Some couples whose tests reveal that nothing is wrong need help in understanding their own reproductive systems. It is amazing that in today's society where sexual permissiveness is the accepted norm many people are as ignorant of basic facts about conception as their forefathers in an age where Victorian prudery militated against any discussion of sexual matters.

They may not even know the time in the woman's cycle when she is fertile. I remember one couple telling me how they had been trying for a baby for a long time without success. Then, because they were contemplating work overseas, they decided that pregnancy would be best deferred. One month later, however, the wife found herself expecting a baby! They had thought that the fertile phase of her cycle was just after and immediately before each period. Therefore, to avoid pregnancy they had restricted intercourse to these particular days of the cycle. Their thinking was confused—for a woman's fertile phase is the middle part of the menstrual cycle rather than just before and after a period.

Aids to fertilization

Finding fertile dates

A woman is fertile around the time when an egg is released from the ovary (ovulation). Fertilization can take place after that. Some women need help in discovering when this part of their cycle occurs. There are several ways this can be done.

If the cycle is regular, periods will occur each month following the same time interval. The date on which the next period is due will then be known and it is easy to calculate when ovulation is likely to take place. Count fourteen days back from when a period is due, and this is usually when ovulation occurs. The fertile phase is for a day or two on either side of this date. (For example, if a period is due on 18th June then the fertile phase is about 2nd to 6th June.)

The second method uses a temperature chart and is slightly more complicated but is usually more accurate. The temperature must be recorded accurately, immediately on waking in the morning, and before doing anything else. The time of ovulation can be seen on the temperature chart by a rise in temperature that was preceded by a fall.

These methods pose obvious problems. Making love may be reduced to a mechanical act, determined more by the date on a calendar or the reading on a thermometer than by desire. It is often wise to use such methods for timing ovulation for a few months only, and then to stop them if pregnancy does not occur. Otherwise considerable tension can build up. The husband may begin to feel like a prize bull, and his wife may be irritable and upset if he doesn't feel like making love at the times she has worked out when she should be ovulating.

Many couples coming into this category do eventually have successful pregnancies. But perhaps the best way of coping meantime is to regard the results of the investigations in a negative light, to assume it is unlikely that there can be a baby and to plan life accordingly. Should pregnancy occur it will then be a wonderful surprise. This acceptance of the likelihood that there can be no pregnancy is probably the antidote to living in an uncertain world under the shadow of a perpetual 'if'.

Sperm counts

For couples where there is a fertility problem with the husband, the diagnosis can usually be made easily. Semen examination is quick to do and an answer will be immediately available. If the result is 'low' or 'zero', then another sample of sperms should be looked at a few weeks later.

Where the testes are permanently damaged (resulting in either very low or zero sperm counts) treatment is rarely successful. Injections of hormones to boost low levels may raise the levels but successful pregnancies following this treatment occur very rarely.

A varicose vein on the testes, however, can often be treated successfully by simple surgery. The sperm count begins to rise after the operation.

Where no obvious reason is found to account

for a low sperm count, simple advice and practical measures may help. Sperms are highly sensitive to heat. Over-exposure to warmth will kill them or reduce their activity. Therefore simple measures like avoiding long hot baths, and not wearing tightly fitting underpants or trousers, can boost the sperm count by removing causes of heat-injury to sperms. A healthy sperm count is not normally affected by baths or trousers, but they may be enough to tip the balance when it is already low.

Many couples worry about the ideal frequency of sexual intercourse and how that may affect the sperm count. Both excessive and infrequent intercourse can affect a sperm count that is already low. If it is low most gynaecologists recommend intercourse no more than alternate nights and at least two or three times a week. This is a rough guide and not an absolute rule!

Where the man produces no sperms at all, the only medical help that can be given is artificial insemination by donor sperm (AID). Anonymously donated sperm specimens are frozen and then stored for use in AID.

Artificial Insemination by Donor

In AID a tiny tube full of donor sperm is gently inserted up through the woman's cervix into her womb when she is ovulating. This is a fairly successful technique with a sperm often fertilizing an egg, although clearly it poses ethical problems (which will be considered later). While the sperms are examined to exclude major genetic abnormalities you cannot know whether your baby may inherit other abnormalities which are more difficult to detect. Another hazard is that the AIDS virus can be transmitted through semen, and a few cases of infection have occurred in Australia from artificial insemination by donor sperm. Until all donors are screened for AIDS, many women will feel the risk of possible infection is too high to run.

Artificial Insemination by Husband

Those for whom an abnormality of the female reproductive system is causing infertility form the group hardest to diagnose and treat. Diagnosis falls into two broad areas—those in whom sperms cannot get to the egg, and those who do not produce or release eggs.

Where 'cervical hostility' is the problem (see previous chapter), the most usual treatment is artificial insemination by husband's sperm (AIH). The husband's sperms are introduced into the wife's womb through a tiny tube going through the mouth of the womb, avoiding contact with the cervical mucus. This is done when the wife is ovulating, and a pregnancy may follow. Sometimes this procedure needs to be repeated during several menstrual cycles before it is successful. It is simple to do and carries no risks.

I personally regard this treatment as legitimate and free of major moral problems for Christians. It simply allows sperms to bypass the mechanical barrier of mucus at the mouth of the womb. It does not in any way break the exclusive commitment of the marriage bond and a baby conceived this way is in all respects the child of both partners.

Some couples thinking about AIH react emotionally to the idea of a doctor being a third person intruding on their exclusive husband/wife relationship and enabling them to conceive a child. You could argue that *any* doctor helping by any method of treating infertility might be called an 'intrusive third person'. But some couples do feel strongly that God has ordained sexual intercourse between husband and wife as the only way in which children are to be produced. Each individual couple must decide for themselves what they are happy to accept, and none should be persuaded into action that is against their consciences.

Where sperms are prevented from reaching eggs by a blockage of the fallopian tubes, there are two possible lines of treatment—surgery and IVF.

In the first of these a relatively major abdominal operation and delicate surgery are involved. The fallopian tubes are tiny and require intricate repair. Even if the blockage is handled successfully the surgery may so damage the tube that it is still unable to perform its basic function of allowing the sperm and egg to meet. Success rates for this operation are not high and the overall risk of abdominal surgery plus the risk of having a general anaesthetic must be considered.

In-vitro fertilization

The other treatment for this condition is in-vitro fertilization (IVF). Controversy and emotions run high when IVF is mentioned—both by those who want the procedure (or parts of it) banned, and by those who see IVF as the only way to enable certain couples to have their own baby and thereby to relieve their heartbreak and sorrow. Because IVF is highly emotive people in both camps tend to over-react without either possessing full facts about the procedure, or fully considering the implications for infertile couples. There is a danger of seeking to ban the procedure totally when certain safeguards and restrictions may be adequate. There is also a danger of adopting the philosophy of 'the end justifies the means' and of disregarding the ethical implications. (These are discussed in chapter 8.)

The thought of test-tube baby techniques conjures up for many people frightening scenes of Frankenstein scientists creating life or even monsters. The reality of IVF is totally different. Doctors and scientists enable the husband's sperms to meet the wife's egg. They then return the fertilized egg back to the wife's womb, hoping that it will implant in the wall of the uterus and will continue to develop successfully. Thus the barrier caused by blocked fallopian tubes will be overcome.

The nickname 'test-tube' derives from the fact that the egg is fertilized outside the body. This is the meaning of 'in vitro' (literally, 'in glass'). Laboratory utensils are used for this procedure, like test-tubes, petri-dishes and microscopes.

Moral problems arise for many people because 'spare embryos' are usually left over which scientists want to examine and experiment on to further their knowledge. Even if they do not experiment on them they still face the problem of how to dispose of unused embryos. Several eggs are removed from the woman's ovary and an attempt is made to fertilize as many as possible. Three or four fertilized eggs are returned into the womb. This may leave several unused embryos. If they were *all* placed in the uterus, then there arises the risk of a large number of them implanting, developing and even miscarrying. The alternatives are to destroy the spare embryos, or to freeze and store them.

The success rate for IVF is low, ranging from ten to fifteen per cent in some new centres to just over twenty per cent in centres with greater experience. Those involved in the procedure aim to increase the chances of initial success, so that ideally the woman will only go through it once.

A laparoscopy is performed to remove the eggs. If only one or two are removed, and neither of them is fertilized by sperms, then another laparoscopy is required before the woman can try again. To avoid repeated surgery, doctors use hormones to stimulate the woman's ovaries to produce more than the customary single monthly egg. They then remove as many as seven eggs (if present) in the hope that three or four of these can be fertilized successfully. Problems arise when *all* the eggs are successfully fertilized.

Experience shows that the best chance of getting one or two eggs to implant in the wall of the womb is to put three or four fertilized eggs in it. The company of the others apparently enhances the possibility of one implanting (or perhaps it simply increases the odds). Implantation—where the egg attaches itself to the wall of the uterus—is unpredictable and one aspect of the procedure over which the doctors have little control. Removing six eggs at laparoscopy ensures the best chance of pregnancy for most women.

While it might seem obvious that all fertilized eggs should be put into the uterus, this poses another problem. Were six embryos to be placed in the womb, the woman would face a high risk of more than one or two implanting—giving a multiple pregnancy (twins, triplets, quins and so on). As the number of eggs that are implanted rises, so the possibility diminishes of the pregnancy continuing normally to full term. The woman becomes more likely to miscarry, or to go into very early labour and have tiny premature babies who cannot survive. Such woman have gone through the IVF procedure, coped with early pregnancy and then suffered miscarriage—all for nothing. This inflicts tremendous emotional trauma.

If ethical dilemmas about IVF could be solved satisfactorily then IVF might be responded to as a remarkable procedure, allowing women who otherwise could never have done so to produce their own babies.

The fertility drug

Finally, the last group of treatments is that which attempts to deal with the situation arising when no egg is produced ready for fertilization. For instance, a small benign pituitary tumour may produce a very high level of the hormone prolactin. This stops ovulation. Treatment is either to remove the tumour or to give the medicine Bromocriptine. This reduces the prolactin level allowing ovulation to occur. In other cases the ovaries fail to function and another medicine, Clomiphene, can be used to stimulate them to work normally and produce eggs again. This medicine used to be called 'the fertility drug' because it sometimes led to quads, quins or even sextuplets! Nowadays, close monitoring and accurate adjustment of the dose given to suit individual patients has lessened the likelihood of more than one fertilized embryo being implanted at any one time.

More complicated problems require more complicated treatment. In some cases the ovaries may be working but neither properly nor adequately. Programmes to correct this may involve hormone injections combined with ultrasound scans and blood samples. Other hormone deficiencies leading to failure in ovulation can be corrected by boosting appropriate hormone levels by injections.

How far is far enough?

These methods all have different success rates, and require different levels of commitment by the patient. Few situations now occur for which some form of treatment cannot be offered. Where no abnormality is detected in a couple, they may be offered the opportunity of IVF. The question now facing the Christian couple is: 'How far should we go in trying to have our own baby?'

One of my friends went through full investigations, had a course of treatment which did not work and was then told that she would never be able to have children of her own (this was before IVF was available as it is today). She and her husband found that verdict hard to accept—but with God's help they did eventually accept it. They applied to adopt a baby and eventually received two children (adoption was easier then than it is now). They adjusted marvellously and are now a happy family. When once I asked her about her inability to have children and how she felt, she replied: 'The Lord has healed me so completely through the gift of these two children that I can hardly remember all the pain.'

In many ways I envied her. I felt I could have coped better with knowing for certain I would not have children. I could have got over all the pain and disappointment in one go, and then adjusted my life either by adopting a baby or by accepting our childless state. The endless courses of unsuccessful treatments I underwent, seemed to do little more than prolong the agony—the build up of hopes, the hormonal see-saw, and the bitter disappointment when the result was failure again.

Once you have embarked on infertility treatment it is very difficult to decide when to call a halt to it, unless there is an obvious reason to do this. You tend to think: 'Perhaps another course of this new drug will work. . . .' To have come so far, and gone through so much and then to give it up makes all your previous efforts appear a total waste of time, energy, emotion, money and other resources.

Of necessity, while you are being treated, your life revolves around the course of treatment to a certain extent—especially if your treatment is complicated, requiring many injections and visits to hospital. It is impossible to forget about your infertility and this may cause great strain on both the husband and wife and sometimes this is reflected in their marriage.

Instead of the husband and wife relationship developing and maturing it may become stunted and impoverished. Instead of their marriage embracing many aspects of life it revolves around only one small, albeit important, area—their desire for children. The husband or wife may begin to feel that they cannot satisfy, or be satisfied, by the other. That marriage is no marriage unless they produce children. Discontent may enter their relationship and grow like a cancer.

Individuality

Each couple must eventually come to a point where they say: 'So far and no further!' This decision in no way implies that previous treatment was a waste. You have tried to have your own child, but now you come to the point where you accept that up to now your medical treatment has failed, and you decide to accept it and to learn to live with it. You cannot go on indefinitely with all the stress and strain of infertility investigations and treatments.

Some doctors continually hold out hope thinking that they are helping their patients by suggesting another course of treatment or a new plan. But false hope is worse than no hope. A time must come when you draw the line and accept that treatments are probably not going to help you. That decision point is different for each couple. Only you and your partner know when that time has come for you.

7

Losing and Finding Hope

Once the cause of my infertility had been diagnosed, treatment was recommended for me. Apparently it had been successful in others whose condition was similar. I was told that I needed to be committed to it as it would involve taking medicines every day plus injections combined with ultrasound scans at times. Harry and I thought about all this carefully and decided to go ahead with it for a few months at least.

I did exactly what I was told to do and had all but given up on it when to my astonishment I discovered I was pregnant. I could not believe it. We were both thrilled. I went round the house floating on air and thanking God a hundred times a day for answering our prayers in this way. I was so happy that I did not mind the sickness or the tiredness one little bit.

Pregnant at last

When I was eight weeks' pregnant I had an ultrasound scan to check that everything was all right.

Everything was fine—right down to my baby's tiny heart beat. I was overjoyed. My first proper antenatal examination was due when I was twelve weeks' pregnant. I would then have another ultrasound scan and so we decided to wait until after that before telling anyone other than family and a few close friends.

The day arrived for my antenatal visit. I felt well and was looking forward to being able to tell everyone our wonderful news.

Both my mother and Harry had offered to take me to the hospital. I had responded: 'There's no point. It's purely routine. I'll be back soon!' But as I drove myself down the motorway the thought suddenly came into my head: 'What will you do if you lose the baby?' A cold shiver ran down my spine. 'No that's impossible,' I told myself. 'God has planned all this so well. The timing is perfect. I feel well and, after all, isn't this God's answer to our prayers? He won't let anything bad happen.'

But the thought persisted and would not go away. So I allowed myself to think about it. I began to wonder: 'Is this baby more important to me than my relationship with God?' I was able to answer: 'No, God is more important to me.' And I turned my thoughts into prayer: 'Nothing could be more important than my relationship with you, Lord. I love you—more than anyone or anything, more than my baby.' I could not know at that point how much those words were to be tested by future events.

I arrived safely at the clinic, and was examined as normal. I noticed that the midwife doing the scan was taking a long time to get a proper picture of the baby. I tried to peer over her so that I could see what was going on. I began to feel uneasy. Surely this investigation was a simple one? What could the problem be? A doctor was called, and my growing apprehension and fears were confirmed. The doctor looked at me and gently told me: 'I'm very sorry . . . but it looks as if your baby has died.'

Shattered hopes

It is amazing how the course of your life can change in an instant. Those few words changed my world. More than that, they shattered it. The reality of those words stunned me. I drove home feeling numb. To my relief Harry was at home. I threw myself into his arms as my feelings boiled over. A flood gate had been opened to despair and tears. Words that had taken only a few seconds to utter had crushed all my hopes and dreams.

I cried and cried. Then I began to express my thoughts: 'Why Lord? How could you do this to me? Why did you let me get pregnant in the first place? I'd already accepted the likelihood that the treatment had probably not worked. I was quite happy and content till you let all this happen.'

I felt terribly frightened. It seemed such a cruel blow. God was in charge of my life and therefore I reasoned that God had done this to me. The possibility that God might actually be cruel was devastating. I thought I knew what God was like and I trusted him. I was swamped by grief and my thoughts were wild and uncontrollable.

I felt dreadful about having to go to the hospital the next day to have my baby removed. But I will never forget the amazing sense I had of God's presence with me at that time. Even though I was mentally yelling abuse at him and was angry at his apparent cruelty to me, he tenderly drew near and it was as if he carried me in his arms through those days. I came round from the anaesthetic with such peace that I knew it was supernatural, and God's gift to me.

Had God failed me?

For days after getting home from hospital I was confused and perplexed. The hardest thing I faced in the whole experience was not losing my baby but feeling that somehow God had let me down. If your husband or close friend lets you down it is hard enough. But how could I cope if God himself really had failed me?

I tried reasoning with myself: 'If I just understood why it happened then I'd be able to cope.'

Each day was dark, despite the beautiful Spring weather. I thought I would never be able to sense joy and happiness again. Depression was a new experience for me. In the past at times I had felt pretty low but this was something different. For the first time I understood how others suffering from depression must feel.

In the past whenever I had been in situations which were sad or difficult I had run straight to God for help and comfort. But now I was unsure whether God would help me. How could I trust him for anything again? I was angry and resentful about the way God had treated me.

My thoughts in the car on the way to the antenatal clinic returned to me. I remembered how I prayed: 'Lord, I love you more than I love my baby—you are more important to me.' Had I prayed honestly and meant what I said or not? Or were those just empty words, spoken because I had been confident that God would never take my baby from me?

Whirlpool of self-pity

During that short pregnancy I had continually come across verses as I read the Bible every day which encouraged me to trust God. Those words had been applicable and special to me and I assumed they meant that everything would be all right—the pregnancy would be successful. But now when I needed the strength and comfort of such words more than ever, my heart and mind were in such turmoil that I could not see or hear anything other than my own grief and sorrow. I was in danger of being sucked down into a whirlpool of self-pity.

Graciously God began to make me aware of what was happening to me. I am sure this was because of the prayers of Harry and many friends. Harry is a minister, and at that time his sermons (though not directed at me) seemed just for me. God began to melt my heart.

Despite all my rebellious thoughts I knew I had nowhere else to turn other than to God. And deep down I really did know that he loved me. I sensed that God whom I had followed for twenty years had not and would not abandon me now.

At this time I read the book *The Cost of Commitment* by Dr John White and found it expressed what God was lovingly beginning to teach me. He writes:

> In suffering, then I give thanks. I give thanks not for the suffering (God is not training me in masochism) but in it. I thank Him that His grace is sufficient. I thank Him that He is well able to deliver me and that in His own time He will. I thank Him that He can turn the suffering to serve His own purposes in my life. I thank Him that because Jesus, as man, suffered more than I ever will, God understands how I feel from personal experience. And as I praise and thank Him I become aware of two things. The suffering lessens. It lessens because the anxiety and fear that accompanied it have gone. (Peace in suffering halves its intensity.) In addition, hope is born as well as a sense of meaning in the suffering. I become almost excited that it will turn to my good. No longer do I wonder how I can bear the suffering. Suffering becomes a sort of chariot on which I ride to new planes of living. (*The Cost of Commitment, John White, Inter-Varsity Press 1976, p.14.).*

God's loving purposes

Perhaps I would never understand why all this had happened to me—some of earth's sorrows will only be explained to us in heaven. But now I was beginning to realize and to believe that God had a purpose in everything that had happened to me. More than that, I began to believe that this was a *loving* purpose.

I was angry that despite feeling God was being cruel, I had no alternative but to turn to him for help. I also knew that I had been a Christian for so long that I could not abandon my Christian faith, it was too important to me. Yet, I resented the fact that I had nowhere else to turn other than to God. No choice was given to me!

Then I realized that the person who had no choice in this was not me but God! Since he had made me a child of his, come what may I knew he would go on loving me as a father continues to love his children no matter what happens to them. God might be disappointed or even angry with me at times but he had promised to love me. His promises are clear in the Bible, so he was lumbered with me! This thought began to thrill me and became the key which unlocked my self-imposed prison isolating me from God.

I looked back over the years and realized ways in which God had cared for, protected, guided, and loved me. I remembered many of the good things he had given me—a wonderful husband, a home, health and strength, and friends who really cared for me. As I began to think like this, the question 'why' became less important to me until I was able to reaffirm the words I had spoken to God in the car: 'Yes Lord, I do love you more than anyone else—more than my baby. Even though I don't understand why, I still trust you.'

Trusting in the dark

I could also see that the persistent theme of trusting God, found in my daily Bible reading during pregnancy, applied to me for now as much as then. I must trust God even in the darkest night of sorrow. I saw too that the thoughts I had had in the car going to the antenatal clinic had been God's gentle preparation for what he knew lay ahead of me.

My pain and hurt did not disappear overnight. Many dark days still faced me but I was proving that God's grace was (as the Bible says) 'sufficient'. I was learning to lean on God and learning to accept his plan for my life. Sometimes I felt that my heart was so broken that it would never mend. But with God all things are possible. He is able to mend even the most broken of hearts—as the psalmist says: 'He heals the broken-hearted and binds up their wounds' (Psalm 147:3).

During the pain and grief it is easy to think: 'I'll never be happy again. My great grief will remain with me for ever and ever, and I'll never get over it.' In one sense you never recover from it but you do learn to cope, to accept and eventually healing will take place within you.

Coming to terms with my loss

It is now more than a year since I lost my baby. Certain times and situations have been very difficult for me. The date when my baby would have been born was one of them. It was difficult to face expectant mothers in the streets. Whenever I went shopping all the pregnant mums in the town seemed to crowd into the same shop as me. It was especially hard if their pregnancy was at the stage that I would have been at had my baby lived.

Insensitive remarks from well-meaning friends hurt very much. People seemed to assume that it had been a relatively minor upset and that I would be back to my normal self in a matter of weeks. Some few months after I lost my baby a friend asked how I was. I opened my heart to her and shared a little of my continuing pain. She seemed surprised that I was still feeling like this and almost shocked that I hadn't got over it completely—and this was around the time my baby would have been due! Unless people have been through an experience like this themselves it is hard for them to realize how devastating it is to lose a baby, or quite how long it takes to come to terms with this form of bereavement! And it is much harder for those who have been longing for a baby for ages and have no assurance that they will ever have another pregnancy.

Yet, I can honestly state now that I am not only contented but also joyful. God has healed my broken heart. The scar remains and perhaps it will persist until I die, but my terrible aching pain has been eased away.

Scars can irritate and mine still flares up from time to time but the nagging pain no longer overwhelms me. This is not because I am superhuman. Far from it! I am aware only too well of my weaknesses and faults. The change in my attitude is something that God has brought about within me.

God's transformations

God promised in the Bible that in *all* things he

works for the good of those who love him (Romans 8:28). I believe this to be true with all my heart. I still do not know why I had to lose my baby—for all I know it might have been abnormal or handicapped in some way. I now see that the *reason* for my loss is not really as important as I once thought it was. I am now confident that God can take *any* situation that is tragic from a human point of view and he can transform it into a platform from which he can display his grace, power and even his great love. God can ultimately bring good out of *any* situation provided we allow him to. We must be willing to let go of all the 'whys' of self-pity, and begin to praise him for the past good he has done for us and for what he can do in and through us in the future. I believe that the best place to bring questions, anger, resentment, and self-pity is right into God's presence in prayer. God knows already how we feel and it is amazing to realize that he understands us so well.

In speaking of Jesus, the Bible explains that 'we do not have a high priest who is unable to sympathise with our weaknesses, but we have one who has been tempted in every way, just as we are—yet was without sin' (Hebrews 4:15).

An immediate result of the loss of my baby was that my maternal instincts had been aroused so much that I now longed for a baby twenty times more than I had before. I had tasted the ambrosia of pregnancy and assumed that God would not have let the medical treatment be successful once if it was not going to work another time. I was impatient to start the treatment and conceive again. There was no question in my mind about whether I would try again or not, the only question was when.

What next?

I was sure the treatment would work immediately—even on the first course. But it didn't work. And it was hard to grasp what was being said after the sixth course of treatment failed: 'There is no point in continuing—it's obviously not going to work this time!' was the medical verdict. Again I agonized with 'whys?'. I could not understand from a medical point of view why the treatment worked the first time but not the second. I did not receive an answer that satisfied my medical mind other than the explanation that 'infertility is a complex business'. I was told that the only option open to us if we wanted a baby of our very own now was in-vitro fertilization.

Harry and I thought and prayed a great deal about this suggestion. Although hope was offered, neither of us felt totally happy about it. We sensed a certain restraint about it, and had no deep peace that it was right for us to go ahead with even more treatment. Our decision not to try IVF is explained in the next chapter.

Yet our decision to stop treatment for infertility was especially difficult for me. Harry was convinced that it was time to call a halt. He felt that my emotions and hormones had received sufficient battering in the last two years, and that I had coped with more than enough.

Our decision was hard to accept at first. It seemed so final. I was still mourning the loss of my baby and now it seemed as if that child would never be replaced by another. However, once a couple of months had passed and my hormones had settled down, I felt like a new woman. I experienced a great release of tension. I was free again—no more treatment, no more visits to the hospital, and no more 'trying for a baby'. As I was able to accept our childlessness, so healing came to me.

My intense longing for a child immediately after losing my baby diminished to a level with which I could cope. I was able now to look towards a future that was not tinged with the sorrow of realizing that we would probably remain childless. I still believe that God is a God who can perform miracles. I do not know what the future holds for me. It is enough for me to know that it is in God's loving hands.

As I look back over the past few years and wonder why all this had to take place in my life, I do not know the answers. But I know I have a new strength, a new dependence on God, and a new capacity to accept his plan for my life as being perfect. I am excited about the future. I know it will not be free from pain but I have proved in experience that God's grace will be sufficient to bring me through anything that may happen to me.

8

What Price a Baby?

Harry and I had to think long and hard before we decided we should call a halt to our pursuit of a baby of our own.

Today's society encourages people to assume they can do anything they want to as long as it makes them feel good and no one else gets hurt by their actions. We are encouraged to grab what we can and to take what we want. The philosophy 'God helps those who help themselves' is widely believed.

The word 'discipline' is increasingly unpopular both in reference to self-discipline or discipline by others. Current culture encourages us to indulge and pamper ourselves and to adopt an attitude of: 'I want, so I must have.'

How we *feel* about something is often taken to be the final arbiter of our actions. External constraints like God-given morality, or moral absolutes, or human wisdom which involves thinking through the logical consequences of certain decisions and actions, have generally been discarded. People today tend to base decisions and actions on their unstable and fluctuating feelings. Such an approach has produced the new ethic which declares: 'If it feels good, do it!' The final outcome of such an ethic is anarchy.

As Christians live in society and are influenced by the culture around them the subliminal effect of this kind of thinking is that many drift from a position of living under the authority of the Bible (God's revealed word) to responding to another authority which is increasingly influenced by feelings. All too frequently I hear people saying: 'But it *feels* right, so surely I can do it?' rather than: 'What does the Bible teach about this, so that I can obey God's word?'

What cost is acceptable?

Christian childless couples need to ask themselves the question: 'How far and for how long should we persist in our attempts to have our own baby? Do we have a right to have a child regardless of the cost?' I believe that 'cost' must be assessed in three ways: the cost in terms of emotional stability, the cost to a marriage, and the cost of being obedient to biblical principles. All three must be considered.

Because infertility treatment has advanced so dramatically there are now few situations in which some form of treatment cannot be offered to help a couple have a baby—though that baby may have the genetic make-up of only one of the partners. Therefore, many Christians feel they can no longer depend on doctors to judge and advise as certainly as in the past. We can no longer say:

'We'll go to the doctor and accept whatever help is available, for as long as it is offered.' The responsibility for making the right decision has now more clearly become a matter of personal choice.

Infertile couples suffer such emotional turmoil that usually they are in no fit state to make major decisions as sensibly as they would at other times, so it is important for Christians to think through the issues, and set deadlines before embarking on infertility treatment. Once you are being treated you are likely to find making rational decisions more difficult than before.

I believe that couples should persist as far and for as long as they can, within the limits of emotional stability, marriage stability and obedience to biblical principles.

The maternal instinct is so strong that some women can be driven on and on to the next and the latest form of treatment. Doctors, reluctant to deny such women the possibility of a child, compassionately continue to offer hope and any possible treatments. The desire to have a baby can consume some women and begin to take over their lives, so that fulfilling the desire for motherhood becomes all absorbing. Many women are unaware of what is happening inside them until it is too late and they are emotional and spiritual wrecks.

People are different with respect to the levels of stress with which they can cope. It is important to know yourself and your limitations. It is even more important that before Christians start on infertility investigations and treatment they should come to God in prayer, seeking his wisdom and guidance. It is equally important to continue to do so throughout all the investigations and treatment. God must always be in control in the lives of Christians—and nothing else (not even having a baby) should be able to usurp that position.

Looking at marriage

Marriage breakdown is escalating and, should present trends continue, one in three marriages will soon be ending in divorce. Christians are not immune from the stress and pressure being exerted on families today. I can think of few stresses on a couple greater than that of unwanted childlessness. This attacks a basic purpose of marriage. The only benefit it produces is that a marriage which successfully survives such stress will emerge the stronger.

The grief and sorrow of childlessness tears many couples apart. Accusations as to which partner is to 'blame', feelings of doubt and insecurity and the nagging query as to whether the other partner could have had children if married to someone else can undermine a couple's union.

Long-term infertility treatment may accentuate the stress and lead to damage in a relationship. Therefore, as couples, we need to honestly face the question: 'What is more important to us—a happy and stable marriage without a family, or a possible damaged or broken relationship striving to get children?' Under severe stress, words said in the heat of the moment may take years to heal.

Children are not the only blessing God gives to a married couple. The Bible refers to them as a 'reward' or 'blessing' but this does not imply that a childless marriage is lacking in many other kinds of blessings. Priorities must be examined prayerfully so that the time to draw the line and call a halt to treatment can be discerned.

Moral issues

The moral issues arising through some forms of infertility treatment have claimed public attention and media debate.

Couples who have started a family without any problems can all too easily make snap judgements about infertility. Knowing very little about treatment other than snippets of information gleaned from TV, magazines or papers, some tend to lump *all* treatments together and claim: 'That's all "unnatural". It's immoral and shouldn't be allowed!' Such thoughtless attitudes cause untold pain to childless couples who (having examined the ethical issues carefully) have decided to have certain treatments which others label as 'unnatural'. Do those who make such pronouncements on treatments like AIH or IVF ever stop to consider the motivation driving an infertile couple to such treatment? Virtually every Christian infertile couple longs to have children 'the natural way', like everyone else. But this is not possible for many of us.

There are many issues on which Christians must take a biblical stand. We must not allow our own desire to blind us. The philosophy that 'the end justifies the means' is never right. And it is vital that facts are correct and theological implications are considered carefully before sweeping statements are made.

God-given principles

I think some forms of infertility treatment should be dismissed as being contrary to God's plan for mankind, because they destroy the marriage bond (Genesis 2:24). Any treatment which involves sperms or eggs of a person other than the marriage partner introduces a third person to the exclusive marriage bond. Although sexual intercourse does not take place a baby conceived like this is not the child of the husband and wife alone. I believe that AID and IVF using either donor egg or sperm breaches the bond of marriage.

Personally, I can see no reason to conceive and give birth to a baby unless it is totally my husband's and mine. The blessing God imparts in giving a couple children is that of joining parts of husband and wife together to form new life.

Good reasons exist for obeying these God-given principles. All sorts of unhappy complications may arise in a situation where the principles are disregarded. The child could be a constant reminder, to the partner who was not the genetic parent, of his or her infertility. If major difficulties arose with that child, the non-genetic parent could deny responsibility on the grounds that the child was not really his or hers. The child could drive a wedge between husband and wife causing untold anguish.

More importantly—what of the child? Is he or she to grow up ignorant of one of his natural parents and uninformed about his full genetic identity? What would a child feel like growing up and knowing that part of him came from an unidentified sperm or egg bank? AID is in this way very different from adoption, where one or both parents are known.

If, for the above reasons, AID is unacceptable to Christians, what about AIH (when the husband's sperms are used to fertilize his wife's egg). In this case, the marriage bond is *not* broken. A child conceived is both the natural and the genetic child of both partners.

Some state that AIH is an 'unnatural' method because sexual intercourse is not the means of bringing sperms and eggs together. On such grounds it could be argued that when a caesarean section is performed to deliver a baby this too is 'unnatural'. Babies were not intended to be born like this! But no one allows a baby, or maybe even both mother and child, to die on the grounds that an operation is 'unnatural', when a caesarean section could save them. A pacemaker keeps a damaged heart beating normally where the 'natural' pacemaker in the heart is faulty. This too could be condemned if 'naturalness' is the guide for action.

Just because something is not done exactly according to the 'natural' method it is not automatically to be ruled out as 'wrong'. Rather the question must be asked: 'Is this breaking any part of God's moral code or not?'

Some would even argue that the doctor who places the husband's sperm in the wife's womb is a third person who is involved in the conception of the child. But after conception following sexual intercourse, doctors are involved in the ante-natal care and delivery of the baby. Is it all right then for doctors to be involved *after* fertilization has occurred but not before? Such arguments defy logic!

I believe that AIH is acceptable *provided* the couple can cope with it emotionally, and are prepared for the commitment involved in hospital visits and so on. I do not believe there are *moral* grounds on which AIH should be unacceptable for Christians.

In-vitro fertilization raises greater controversy, even laying aside for a moment the problems of research on 'spare embryos' and their disposal. Is there any ethical objection to straightforward IVF when the husband's sperm fertilizes the wife's egg outside the body, and is then replaced in the womb?

This takes 'doctor interference' a step further than AIH. Some people appear to assume that doctors are creating life by this technique. But God alone creates life itself. Doctors can do no more than create a *situation* in which it is possible for life to be created—by giving sperms the opportunity of fertilizing eggs. Fertilized eggs are then replaced in the wife's uterus for life to develop further.

Some argue that a child is a gift from God and that AIH and IVF turn the child from being a gift into a 'product'—manufactured to order by the procreational scientists.

Yet, I would query whether life is less of a gift because its attainment has involved effort. Is it less of a gift because it has been long and painfully awaited and sought with great intensity of desire? Do these factors make it of greater or lesser value to the recipients?

Precious life so avidly sought may be viewed by its parents as a special gift precisely because they are dependent on God to entrust them with life! They accept help from procreational scientists but realize that anybody conceived by extraordinary means is a very wonderful God-given gift.

I would suggest that sometimes babies who are conceived easily or 'by accident' are those who tend to be seen as 'products' or as unwanted gifts 'forced' on a mother. Couples who conceive easily generally use contraception and time the arrival of their babies to suit them. They are able to prevent pregnancy, and have control of the situation unlike infertile couples who must wait for God's timing. Couples who use birth control carefully are more likely to view their children as being the products of their actions. Each baby is 'their child' —they planned its conception and timed its birth without necessarily waiting for God's timing. This can be argued to be as 'unnatural' as AIH or IVF, but does that make it wrong?

Priorities and resources

Sadly another objection some raise against treatment of infertility is that limited public resources are needed for life-saving procedures. Treatment of illnesses must have priority, and the conquest of injury and prevention of disease should come first.

This argument can be used against any minority group like handicapped people, those with rare diseases or patients kept alive by kidney machines. Who is to decide which people are worth the use of public resources and which should be denied them? Only those who are ignorant of, or callous about, the crushing agony infertility causes could dismiss such couples as 'not worthy of public funds'. I would argue that many infertile couples give more money to society than most others since both husband and wife tend to be employed and pay income tax at full rates. They do not receive child benefits, tax relief for children, or free prescriptions. They contribute to all these allowances which couples having children receive. They are more available and often more willing to help in voluntary work in society. It seems paradoxical that others may want to deny them financial assistance that could help correct an abnormality causing them heartbreak.

I agree that public funds should not be diverted from vital medical facilities nor used for dubious treatment of infertility, but I believe that money should not be withheld from improving NHS infertility treatment services.

I would like to see a wider provision of NHS infertility clinics, staffed adequately by caring medical teams. I would like to see counselling facilities attached to such clinics. Clinics should be organized and equipped so that couples can attend without lengthy waits or fear of embarrassment or feeling they are being processed like objects on a conveyor belt. I would like to see more senior gynaecologists being trained and appointed to specialize in such clinics so that couples do not have to see a different junior doctor every time they attend. I would like to see more care being expended on couples who are deeply hurt by their situation and emotionally fragile.

God's will for each individual

So am I saying that I see no objections to IVF? I believe that IVF is a remarkable technique which can give certain infertile couples the opportunity of trying to have their own children, and so removing much distress. However, serious ethical problems arise with IVF and it is therefore vital for each Christian couple to understand God's will for them personally, and to be confident that this is God's way for them before embarking on this particular treatment.

'Spare' embryos

The ethical problem of what is to be done with the tiny human lives contained in 'spare' embryos requires serious consideration. Those who argue that scientists should be allowed within limitations to do virtually what they want to with these 'spare' embryos (discard them or experiment on them to further man's knowledge), would say that they are not completely alive at such an early stage of development.

The argument as to when life begins raises many complex if not unanswerable questions. The Bible clearly shows that God is interested in people even before they are conceived. As Christians look back they can state: 'God knew me even before the foundation of the world. He chose me in him before the creation of the world . . .' (see Ephesians 1:4). But, of course, it remains true that not every fertilized egg develops into a baby. Nature herself discards thousands and we cannot know which of them God has ordained to develop into children and which he has not. This is holy ground because life is a mystery to finite human minds, and God alone is the one with the power to impart or withhold life.

Where there is any degree of doubt about when life begins, should we therefore assume the right of deciding which fertilized eggs will have an opportunity to live and which will not? Is not that the prerogative of God alone? I believe that it is not for us to decide to destroy several lives in order to attempt to create another one.

What about experimentation on 'spare' embryos? If it is agreed that they should not be discarded then it follows that experimenting on them is an even greater evil. I believe that allowing experimentation in any form, and at any stage, on the life of an embryo is to open the floodgates to evil. Some of those who argue that experimentation is necessary to perfect IVF techniques so that more infertile couples can be helped may use this as an emotional lever to attain other aims of their own. But IVF is an established technique and it does not require experimentation on embryos to further it, or to allow it to continue.

Compassion

Compassion was one of the motives behind the 1967 Abortion Act—compassion for women with genuine reasons for wanting an abortion. It was reasoned that this would stop women from going to backstreet abortionists and suffering the potential horrors of infection, haemorrhage and even death.

Few people foresaw the results today of such a 'compassionate' law. An appalling situation now exists where abortion is available virtually on demand. A common reason now for an abortion is that a baby would be an inconvenience. One baby is now aborted every two to three minutes in Britain—a legal form of mass murder! Women requiring important gynaecological surgery have to wait many months because operating theatres are blocked by women having abortions. This situation came about as a result of compassion for women with 'unwanted' pregnancies.

Now further legislation is being drafted that springs apparently from compassion for the infertile—legislation that would permit research on human embryos.

Those who proclaim loudly that childless couples should be treated with compassion are often those who demand compassion for women wanting abortion on demand. How can the two be compatible?

I believe that the infertile are in danger of being exploited—of being used as the reason for certain practices which could not possibly please God. It is easier to gain public support and sympathy for an emotional cause than simply to state: 'We want to further scientific knowledge.' Yet, the very people they claim they want to help (childless people like me) will probably be those who will benefit least. I sometimes wonder whether those running infertility clinics and IVF programmes are half as interested in the emotional hurts of their patients as they are in their own research.

Probably the most effective way in which infertile couples could be helped would be by major changes in the abortion laws. Instead of all those babies being killed they could be allowed to live and be placed for adoption. Couples like Harry and I would love to be able to adopt a baby.

I believe that IVF is still an option open to Christian couples provided safeguards are somehow guaranteed to protect 'spare' embryos. It is impossible, though, to visualize how this could ever be guaranteed. And yet, many different reasons combined to dissuade Harry and I from accepting IVF for ourselves. We had to carefully weigh up the cost to us in terms of our emotional stability, our marriage, the fate of our 'spare embryos' and our desire to obey biblical principles.

Our decision

After all the investigations and treatment I received, then my pregnancy and loss of my baby, then yet more treatment which failed, I probably had reached my emotional limit. I doubt whether I could have coped with further bitter disappointment had IVF failed for us, or worse still had it succeeded and I then had another miscarriage.

The chances of success were slim—I was told about fifteen per cent.

Probably our marriage had weathered enough with all the treatment programmes. We needed to return to a normal marriage routine and enjoy freedom from these abnormal pressures.

Finally we decided that we were not totally happy with IVF for ourselves. I would have insisted that every fertilized egg must be replaced in my womb. Yet I wondered if I could be totally confident that no mistakes would be made when I could not watch what was happening to my eggs and Harry's sperms all the time.

Suppose my insistence meant that an abnormal embryo was placed in my womb? How would I feel? Suppose it meant replacing six fertilized eggs, and running the risk of multiple pregnancy?

The final deciding factor was seeing someone on TV who had just given birth to six premature babies. I'm not sure if all or any of them survived, but the thought of having six babies at the same time appalled me. It would mean spending most of the pregnancy in hospital. If the babies survived, then our entire lives would revolve around them. I could not run such a risk. Harry and I did not believe that God was calling us to dedicate our lives to bringing up four or more babies. I had read of one husband who gave up his job to help his wife look after their sextuplets. That did not seem right for us—I could never expect, nor would I ever want, my husband to give up his job as a minister in the church. We decided together that the way in which IVF would be acceptable to us was a way which involved risks too great for us to take.

We decided then that we had reached the end of the line. We were not prepared for the cost of proceeding any further with treatment.

I believe that God has honoured our decision. I have not miraculously become pregnant, but God has given us a sense of peace, of contentment and of joy about this whole issue.

9
The Adoption Option

'If someone really wants a baby, why not just adopt one?' a friend once asked me rather aggressively.

Sadly, many others share this attitude. People seem to think that adoption is as easy as driving down to the local supermarket and selecting the baby of your choice. While adoption may appear to be an uncomplicated alternative to having your own children, it is far from easy.

Those Christians who have successfully adopted babies often testify that through the gift of someone else's children God has healed their own heartbreak, bringing joy to their lives. Their sense of shame and failure has been removed. Others, though they love their adopted children dearly and are somewhat comforted, still remain painfully conscious of their failure to produce children of their own—especially if they are able to adopt only one child.

No alternative to childlessness is totally painless or simple. Couples can never escape the reality of their infertility even though they may be fulfilled to some extent by adopting, or fostering, or by other means.

Difficult process

I first realized that adoption was a difficult process about three years ago. My gynaecologist explained that if I was going to try to adopt children (should the infertility clinic fail) then I ought to set the wheels in motion without delay. He told me that adoption waiting lists were long and I might have to wait as long as five years before a baby was available for me. These words 'five years' seemed like an eternity. I could not believe that anyone would have to wait so long for a child.

This shocked Harry and me into thinking through our feelings about adoption. Should we or shouldn't we apply? We had shelved the matter up to this point, leaving it at the back of our minds as our last ditch attempt to have a family should all else fail. We had never seriously considered the possibility that we might not be accepted as suitable to be adoptive parents, or once accepted that there could be several years' delay before we held our own baby in our arms.

We started to think this through together. We could see several possible reasons why God might want us to remain childless. We would have more time for church work. It is easier to have an 'open home' for friends and people in need if you have no children. We still had a spare room in which visitors could stay. I was not occupied by looking after little children, and so there was more free time for church activities, for entertaining and for helping and supporting Harry in my role as a minister's wife. Although I had never put furthering my career in medicine very high up my priority list, it was a possibility more open to me if I remained childless.

Despite this, neither of us could deny our strong desire to have children, even if they were not our own. We reasoned that surely if God intended us to remain childless, he would give us the grace and desire to accept this?

Advantages of adoption

We considered the advantages of adoption. We felt we could offer a secure loving home to a baby who was otherwise unwanted. We could perhaps even offer such a home to a toddler or older child who had suffered abuse or ill treatment. Not only did we long to be parents but we could see that having children of our own would be an advantage in our role in the church. Childless couples can be very naïve about family problems. Not only would we be able to empathize with those who could not have their own children, but after adopting we could help others through their ups and downs in rearing a family.

The fact that remained most persistent was that we really *did* want children. But whether this was the least important factor or the most important in our decision-making, that was the difficult question! Our wanting a family did not give us a right to have one—and yet for us to cope with the major upheaval such a child would bring, we knew we would really have to desire it.

We could see that our life-style, minus the cares of bringing up children, was relatively straightforward and orderly; and we liked it that way. We had time for each other and we enjoyed that. Could we cope with sleepless nights, toys all over the place, lack of freedom and privacy? These were important matters to be considered. We were not so naïve as to assume that life with a child would be plain sailing! But eventually after a great deal of prayer and thought we decided to explore the possibility of adoption without yet committing ourselves.

Facing hard issues

We discovered we had unexpected hang-ups about adoption which needed working through. And then there was the question of the age of children we would go for, should we finally plan to adopt. Babies are in short supply and waiting lists for them are long. Toddlers and older children desperately needing homes usually come with suitcases full of problems inherited from disturbed backgrounds. Such children could well present peculiar behaviour patterns and be difficult to handle.

I began to face issues which hitherto had not been matters of concern. I worried, saying to myself: 'He won't look like us—it will be so obvious that he's not ours!' My social worker tried to encourage me by saying that it is uncanny how often adopted children grow to be like their adoptive parents—assuming their mannerisms and expressions. A friend shared her experience of a holiday camp with her two adopted children. Her husband and adopted son entered a father and son look-alike competition. To their amazement they won second prize!

'Would we really think of him or her as "ours"?' I asked another friend. 'Honestly, I never think of mine as being adopted,' she replied. 'I even have to remind myself that I didn't give birth to them. Surely the real parents are those who love and bring up a child.'

'Suppose we get a child who is dull and unintelligent?' Harry and I asked ourselves—only to realize that academic attainment is not really important. If we could make a child happy and secure, help him to be as healthy as possible, and encourage him to develop whatever gifts he had, then we felt we would be contributing something important to his development. The vital gift we could give a child would be to share our knowledge of God with him.

'But what if he rebels against everything we hold dear? Suppose he doesn't even want to go to church when he grows up?' we asked ourselves. 'What if it was a total disaster?'

We had heard horror stories of adopted children who went their own way, breaking the hearts of their adoptive parents. But we had also heard similar horror stories where children who had not been adopted did exactly the same thing! Such fears are part of Christian parenthood.

Trusting God

At this point it was very clear that we were not trusting God totally about all this. While it was important to face potential problems realistically the most important issue for us as Christians was whether it was *God's* plan for us to adopt a child. If we were in the business of committing each step of the adoption process to God in prayer, and were willing for him to redirect us or stop us at any stage, then surely we could trust him to work things out for the best?

Sometimes a little voice whispered in my heart: 'Don't be fooled. It might turn out wrongly. God allows things to be bad at times. He might have a few heartbreaks in store for you.' Just before I panicked about such a possibility I realized I had lessons to learn through all this and asked God to show me what they were.

I realized I needed to trust God completely. I had to be willing to follow God's plan for me rather than what I thought his plan should be. I would love to have a beautiful intelligent trouble-free child who brought us nothing but joy. But I could see that this was not necessarily God's plan for us. His plan could entail many difficulties and heartaches along the way. Should things apparently turn out disastrously, I needed to be able to face the question I knew would spring to mind: 'Have we made an awful mistake?'

If we adopted a child believing this was God's purpose for us, then I must be willing to accept the child he sent. God would ensure the child of his choice came to us. He would not guarantee trouble-free times but through every problem that arose he would help us and give us the wisdom we needed to handle it.

Fear of rejection

And yet I still had anxious moments over another facet of the issue. 'Suppose we are rejected by the adoption society?' I thought. Can we face another closed door, another disappointment? Then I remembered one of the lessons God had taught me earlier. When I first considered infertility investigations I had been afraid of going ahead for many different reasons. Fear almost paralysed me and prevented me from doing anything. I could see a similar situation might arise here. Fear of rejection and failure could lead us to inaction. Would we later regret this?

Those who decide against adoption do so for many different reasons. Some find the hassle of applying, the invasion of privacy during assessment, and the fear of ultimate rejection overwhelming. 'Better leave things alone,' they reason. I remember an elderly widow sharing with me the story of her life and the happy times she had with her husband. Then her face clouded and her voice was full of regrets: 'We never had any children. We thought about adoption but never got round to it. . . .'

For some others, the stumbling-block to adoption is pride or stubbornness. Someone else told me bitterly: 'I'd have adopted but Jim wouldn't hear of it. He said if we couldn't have our own children then we wouldn't have any.'

I do not believe that every childless Christian couple should try to adopt a child but I think each should at least think through the questions: 'What does God want us to do with our lives? What special thing could we do if we remain childless? Is adoption God's plan for us?'

Our decision

In the end, Harry and I decided to apply for adoption of a child in the under-five age group as we knew that the waiting list for toddlers was shorter than for babies.

We waited several weeks after our assessment to hear whether we had been accepted. Those weeks were like several years. When the news came that we had been accepted as adoptive parents we were overjoyed thinking that soon we would have a child. It was just a matter of waiting for the right one. A few weeks later a friend told me she was pregnant. I wanted to respond: 'I'm sort of pregnant too . . . I'm expecting a child any week now!' Although we told very few people that we were planning to adopt I was very excited about it.

At that stage we did not realize that my 'pregnancy' would last so long! We had been told that a toddler would be placed with us without a long delay—but that was nearly three years ago and at the stage of writing this we are *still* waiting!

Everyone knows something of disappointment in their lives but to some infertile couples it begins to feel as if life is nothing but disappointments.

Disappointed again

There is the disappointment of failing to conceive as quickly as you had planned. Then the monthly disappointment as each period reminds you that you are still not pregnant. Disappointments occur again and again with infertility investigations and treatment. There is further sadness when miscarriages occur, and disappointment yet again when you try to adopt. Rising hopes and fading disappointments are part of the pattern of infertility.

How true it is that 'hope deferred makes the heart sick' (Proverbs 13:12). For me one major area of learning and growth in recent years has had to be the issue of coping with constant disappointments. It has been imperative to know more of the Lord who 'heals the broken-hearted and binds up their wounds' (Psalm 147:3).

As a student I was hurt once by a traumatic broken romance. My minister at the time helped me with words I have never forgotten. He said: 'God, having some better thing for you, has allowed this.'

At the time I thought: 'He doesn't know what he's talking about. He doesn't know how hurt I am. My heart can never be mended. What could possibly be "a better thing" for me?' But eight months later I met Harry—God's perfect husband for me. I now have no regrets that my first romance broke up!

That taught me an important lesson. Since then whenever I have faced disappointment I have remembered these words and proved them true *every* time.

God does not permit needless tears. He can take each disappointment, each broken heart and heal it. He can use disappointment to lead us into his good and perfect plan for our lives.

I recall being quite hurt by one friend who implied that adopting a child was a 'second best', that this was to be accepted because what you really want is unattainable. She was wrong! If adopting a child is God's plan for me then how can I regard it as 'second best'? God's plans for us are perfect and good. We receive 'second best' only if, and when, we disobey him deliberately.

Adoption not possible?

Suppose adoption is not an available option to you. What can you do? Earlier this year I was frustrated by the length of time being taken to have a child placed with us. I decided to see whether any other adoption agencies would be quicker. The first replied: 'Sorry you're outside our area.' The next said: 'We've been closed for some time.' The third agency was the one in whom I placed my hopes. I knew they were very efficient, and that once accepted by them a child would be placed quickly. I approached them with excitement—unprepared for their reply: 'Sorry, you're too old!' With Harry being thirty-seven and myself thirty-three I felt this was rather an exaggeration.

Adoption agencies have strict criteria for selecting adoptive parents because of the high numbers of prospective parents and the limited number of babies available.

The burden of infertility is made heavier to bear because of current difficulties in adopting. Childless couples nowadays are almost forced to go to great lengths if they really wish to have a child in the family because they know that unless they can have a baby themselves by *some* means (surrogacy, donated egg or sperm, etc), they will never have a family.

Ten years ago it was relatively easy to adopt one or two babies. Now you are extremely fortunate if you are able to adopt just one baby.

And the reasons are not difficult to find. A primary factor is that abortion is so readily available.

The issue of abortion clearly impinges upon the predicament which childless couples face. The moral issues and dilemmas which surround the subject of abortion are bound to be viewed with added intensity by those who long for and cannot have children of their own. While of course the Christian arguments against abortion are arguments of principle (based on the Bible's view of the sanctity of life) rather than of expediency, it is worth remembering that there are many childless couples who would eagerly give a loving secure home to an unwanted child rather than contemplate that child's life being terminated before it has even seen the light of day.

Another reason why it is so difficult nowadays to adopt a child, lies within society's increased acceptance and in some measure support for single parent families.

Exploring fostering

When a girl opts not to have an abortion and to keep her baby she may do a marvellous job of taking care of her little one, accepting her responsibility and providing adequate love and security. However, some see the baby as a ticket to State benefits and council housing, or as a live doll to be played with. Problems arise if the baby's cries do not stop. Some end up being abused or maltreated at the hands of Mother's boyfriend, or even by the fraught mother herself. Those reaching media headlines are but the tip of the iceberg. If the child is fortunate, the NSPCC and social services will step in to try to end the baby's misery—but it is not easily terminated. A child may go from foster home to foster home and eventually land in a residential home. If the child is fortunate he may be adopted by a couple who will really love him.

Christians should be in the forefront of taking some of these emotionally damaged and scarred children into their families, giving them love and security.

This is a difficult task. You must consider it carefully and go into it only once you are fully aware that there will be problems. Many children have behaviour problems. Some will not yet be toilet trained. Some may use language that embarrasses or offends you. Adjustment for parents and child may be very hard for many months. Legal battles may have to be fought to gain consent to adopt the child. But this could be part of God's plan for some who are childless. We have a beautiful example to follow in thinking of our Father God who has adopted us and made us members of his family. When God adopted us we were no more loveable than some of these very disturbed little ones!

Staying as a twosome

Don't feel guilty if you decide that adopting or

fostering is not for you. You may genuinely feel that if you are unable to have your own children that you would be better staying as you are. Accept your ability to be content with your situation as a gift from God.

But what of those who have made up their minds that they do want to adopt and who are rejected because of age, medical or social reasons? What of those of us who continue to wait—hoping that one day a child will be placed with us—while the hoping and the waiting seem to simply stretch on for ever?

God's best for us

This is a situation in which my trust in God is tested to its limit. Do I really believe that God is in charge of my life? Do I believe he has a plan for me? Do I believe that he times events in my life perfectly? Or do I think things happen haphazardly? Do I believe that I am really at the mercy of the social services?

In this situation I have applied lessons learned in the past about disappointment and trusting God when I cannot see in the dark. Despite this I am still human enough to ask from time to time: 'But what is it all for?'

I am confident that when we sincerely seek God's will for us, and try to obey him, he will guide us into his good and perfect will. I am sure that God's timing *is* perfect.

I may not know what God is doing but I do believe that eventually we will be able to see God's hand in all the events of our lives. God has a special purpose for your life and for mine. Our job is constantly to seek it. If we have no children then God can use our childlessness to do something very special. Our great God brings good out of sad and tragic situations. He cares about us, feels for us in our pain and sadness, and wants to lead us into abundant life.

If God has closed the door of adoption to you and me then he means to open another door. That door will not open to reveal something second or third best. It will be God's *very best* for us!

10

To Be Continued

I am increasingly convinced that no matter what circumstances Christians find themselves in, Jesus intends each one of us to experience rich and full lives.

We will not necessarily be happy all the time and certainly life will not be free from varying degrees of trouble and pain. But Jesus Christ can supply us with all we need to give our lives purpose and direction, fulfilment and joy.

This quality of joy for the Christian is more than mere happy or pleasant feelings. It is a deep sense of contentment. It is such that even in the middle of sorrow and pain the Christian can amazingly still know joy. Such joy springing from the knowledge and trust that God will bring the Christian through each trial means we can rest content that God has his own purpose for our suffering and is going to bring good out of it ultimately.

The secret of contentment

Is such contentment the automatic experience of each Christian? Can we pray for it at night and wake up the next morning to find it is ours?

The Apostle Paul speaks of the way in which he found this secret: 'For I have learned to be content whatever the circumstances' (Philippians 4:11). How did he learn to experience such contentment? It became his as he learned to draw on Christ's strength in every circumstance throughout his Christian life.

He goes on to state: 'I know what it is to be in need, and I know what it is to have plenty. I have learned the secret of being content in any and every situation, whether well fed or hungry, whether living in plenty or in want' (Philippians 4:12).

What is the secret of attaining what seems almost impossible for us? Paul's secret is Jesus—'I can do everything through him who gives me strength' (Philippians 4:13). Jesus was the source of his strength and ability to find contentment despite adverse circumstances. His contentment lay in Christ himself and not in the circumstances of his own life.

We too can experience such God-centred contentment, and grow and mature as Christians and as people in the process. Coming to terms with infertility is hard. Such a deep personal disappointment, and the depths of pain and anguish it causes, can only be fully understood by those who have faced this particular form of suffering.

Yet others have also faced equally painful and

distressing situations. Joni Eareckson was only seventeen when she was paralysed from the neck down by an accident while swimming. In her first book *Joni* she shared the way in which she had to learn to come to terms with her accident and paralysis. In her second book *A Step Further* she wrote of some of the lessons God taught her through what had happened to her.

She says:

> Today as I look back, I am convinced that the whole ordeal of my paralysis was inspired by God's love. I wasn't a rat in a maze. I wasn't the brunt of some cruel divine joke. God had reasons behind my suffering, and learning some of them has made all the difference in the world. (Pickering and Inglis 1979, p.14).

Understanding some of the reasons for our personal suffering can help us to be contented and to trust God. It has certainly helped me to realize that I am not the plaything of a cruel uncaring God, but rather all that happens in my life springs out of God's tremendous love for me.

Learning from others

At times I've had to take myself in hand and remember that having no children is not the end of the world. I've had to make myself face the reality of the fact that in spite of my great personal unfulfilled longing, my life has fallen in very pleasant paths compared with the lot of countless others.

Recently I re-read a book which had inspired me in my early Christian life. It was about the

Scottish Covenanters. They were people who willingly suffered cold, hunger, loneliness, pain and torture, and many were killed for the cause and glory of Christ. I felt ashamed of the times I had wallowed in self-pity over my childlessness. Their example has reminded me again of the many blessings in my own life.

Life constantly presents us with choices to be made. God did not create us as robots to do his bidding. He wants us to have a close and intimate relationship of love with him. Therefore, he has given us the freedom to choose or reject this.

In the matter of self-preoccupation there are choices to be made. Of course we can become over-sensitive and easily hurt, believing that almost everything anyone says to us is a deliberate attempt to wound us. We can become so turned in on ourselves that we are blinkered and blind to the blessings God lavishes on us, and also to the fact that other people have their own problems. But we have a choice. We do not need to be like that or to remain in that self-orientated state for ever.

We are able to choose whether we will continue to indulge our self-pity and turn into spiritual paupers, or rather seek God's help to deliver us from self-pity's hold on us. If self-pity is enthroned in our hearts then it needs turning out and Christ must be returned to his throne. As we do this, we will begin to learn how to be contented, and this in turn brings acceptance and healing for our hearts.

Although Jesus is able to help us do this we must be willing to accept his help, even if it proves painful. Sometimes we ask God to deal with specific sins like pride, self-pity or selfishness. But when he answers us, and his corrective surgery begins, we draw away from the pain it necessarily causes.

In his book *The Great Divorce* C. S. Lewis illustrates how we desire God to change us into his likeness and yet are at the same time reluctant for it. He writes of an angel and a ghost-like creature with a red lizard on his shoulder at the outskirts of heaven.

> 'Off so soon?' said a voice.
>
> 'Yes I'm off,' said the ghost. 'Thanks for all your hospitality. But it's no good, you see. I told this little chap (here he indicated the lizard) that he'd have to be quiet if he came—which he insisted on doing. Of course his stuff won't do here: I realise that. But he won't stop. I shall just have to go home.'
>
> 'Would you like me to make him quiet?' said the flaming spirit—an angel, as I now understood.
>
> 'Of course I would,' said the ghost.
>
> 'Then I will kill him,' said the angel, taking a step forward.
>
> 'Oh—ah—look out! You're burning me. Keep away,' said the ghost, retreating.
>
> 'Don't you want him killed?'
>
> 'You didn't say anything about killing him at first. I hardly meant to bother you with anything so drastic as that.'

The conversation goes on:

> 'May I kill it?
>
> 'Honestly, I don't think there's the slightest necessity for that. I'm sure I shall be able to keep it in order now. I think the gradual process would be far

better than killing it.'

'The gradual process is of no use at all.'

'Get back! You're burning me. How can I tell you to kill it? You'd kill me if you did.'

'It is not so.'

'Why, you're hurting me now.'

'I never said it wouldn't hurt you. I said it wouldn't kill you.' (Fontana 1972, p.89 ff.)

Finally the ghost allows the angel to kill the lizard and then the ghost is totally transformed into an immense real man.

Pain has a purpose

When we allow God to deal with specific sins in our lives, he may choose to do so by allowing us to go through painful experiences. But we will afterwards realize that the reward was well worth the pain.

As the New Testament says: 'For our light and momentary troubles are achieving for us an eternal glory that far outweighs them all' (2 Corinthians 4:17).

For some of us the painful experience of childlessness is part of God's special surgery in our lives. Have you ever thought of childlessness as an opportunity rather than a burden? It can be a wonderful opportunity for us to grow as Christians. It can be an opportunity for us to display God's power and glory in our lives as we learn to cope with being childless. It can also be an opportunity for God to mould and change us and to make us more like Jesus.

When I first thought of my childlessness in this

light I fell to my knees to thank God. Instead of my situation hanging over me like a black cloud it became a door that opened onto opportunity. I wondered what God could or would do with my life—and this was exciting. What glorious purposes had he planned for me?

As I began to look for any benefits that were mine as a childless married woman, I was amazed to discover there were many advantages. I began to look on it positively rather than negatively. Instead of moaning that I had no children I could enjoy the freedom this gave. I have wasted time and energy dwelling on God's denial of children rather than accepting this fact as coming from a loving Father who knows what is best for me. I began to see that God wanted my life to go in a different direction. It was a direction that would be no less wonderful for being childless because it was God's very best plan for me.

I quietly realized that my marriage to Harry was stronger and more beautiful because of the time we had been able to spend with each other giving one another undivided attention. There had been years of getting to know one another far more deeply than we could have done had we had a baby. We had done things together, learned together and helped support each other through difficult times.

I saw many young mums stuck at home with little children while Dad went to all sorts of interesting places. I noticed that some were resentful and bitter at being tied to the house. Some did not conceal their envy of my freedom and at times even made me feel guilty about enjoying it!

Yes, there are positive advantages in being childless if we only look for them. Perhaps we should call it 'child-free' instead of 'childless'.

The greatest benefit to me in having no children is that this experience has taught me much about myself that I could have learned no other way. God has used the actual experience of being childless and of learning to cope with it to help me grow as a woman and also as a Christian.

I have also learned more of the tremendous height and depth of God's love for me personally, to an extent I think I could not have known otherwise. I have discovered that God is far more concerned about *me* as a person than about anything I *do* for him. He is more concerned about shaping me so that I become more like Jesus and achieve my full potential as a Christian, than he is about giving me presents that will make me love him.

When we bribe children, trying to make them love us by giving them presents and privileges it does not work. They merely expect more presents! They learn to love the gifts rather than the giver!

It is like this with God. He is able to give us our heart's desire but this would not make us love him more. We would love the gifts rather than the Giver. When God gives us gifts and blessings they are tokens of his love for us, not to make us love him. In fact, it is often when God withholds gifts and blessings from us that he teaches us to love and depend on him. Suffering is an opportunity to demonstrate our loyalty to God even in the most difficult times. If our love depends on what we can gain from God, then it is not true love but it is rather love of self.

When God disciplines us he does so because he is our loving Father. He wants us to be the best we can be. He wants us to be holy. God is preparing us for an eternity with himself, not for a life-time of service here (although he does give us that privilege).

When a great artist is painting a picture he works on it for a very long time—constantly changing, adding and removing until it is a thing of beauty. Only then will he sign his name to it and allow it to be displayed in a gallery. Heaven is God's display room for his saints.

At the time of Joni Eareckson's accident, many people thought: 'What a tragedy—a young life completely ruined—what will she do?' Joni had two choices. She could give in to the tragedy and live a life of bitterness and resentment. Her life would then have been truly ruined—not by the accident but by her response to it. The other alternative was for her to ask God for help in learning to cope with her situation. She chose the latter.

Her attitude to her suffering is summed up in her own words:

> When God brings suffering into your life as a Christian, be it mild or drastic, He is forcing you to decide on issues you have been avoiding. He is pressing you to ask yourself some questions. Am I going to continue trying to live in two worlds, obeying Christ and my own sinful desires? Or am I going to refuse to worry? Am I going to be grateful in trials? Am I going to abandon my sins? In short am I going to be like Christ? (Joni Eareckson and Steve Estes, *A Step Further* Pickering and Inglis 1979, p.77.)

Our response to our suffering is vitally important

to our Christian growth. How we respond is our personal choice.

Serious business

Living with Christ as Lord of our lives is not a game which we can play or discard as we choose. Submitting ourselves to his loving will is the serious business of the Christian life. Many Christians wonder why they do not experience the power and joy of Christ. Often this is because they are only playing at being Christians. Their pleas for Christ to be Lord of their lives are half-hearted and not really serious. I was probably like this before learning to cope with childlessness. This made me realize that giving my all to Christ means *all*. He was either Lord of all, or Lord of virtually nothing.

It is easy to sing words like 'I all on earth forsake'. It is not difficult to think and honestly (though ignorantly) tell God: 'I am willing to give up everything for you. All I am and all I have is yours.' But sometimes God has to teach us that the three letter word *all* is a very comprehensive word.

When I finished reading one of Joni's books I thought: 'If she hadn't had her accident she would probably have lived an ordinary life and her Christian life might have been pretty shallow. But through God, and her response to her accident, she has become a mature Christian woman. God has enabled her to reach her fullest potential. Through her painting, poetry, singing, writing and speaking she has blessed, encouraged, and challenged thousands if not millions of people.'

Before I knew I would be childless I asked God to take my life and to make me more like Jesus. Soon I was plunged into all sorts of difficulties—of which one was our unfulfilled desire for children. I could not understand why God was allowing pain in so many different areas of my life.

I was helped when I came across some verses written by John Newton, the one-time slave trader whose conversion to Christ catapulted him into a fruitful ministry. Newton knew much about suffering—including childlessness. He wrote:

I asked the Lord that I might grow
In faith, and love, and every grace;
Might more of His salvation know,
And seek more earnestly His face.

I hoped that in some favoured hour
At once He'd answer my request,
And, by His love's constraining power,
Subdue my sins and give me rest.

Instead of this, He made me feel
The hidden evils of my heart,
And let the angry powers of hell
Assault my soul in every part.

Yea, more, with His own hand He seemed
Intent to aggravate my woe;
Crossed all the fair designs I schemed,
Blasted my gourds, and laid me low.

Lord, why is this? I trembling cried,
Wilt Thou pursue Thy worm to death?
''Tis in this way,' the Lord replied,
'I answer prayer for grace and faith.

'These inward trials I employ
From self and pride to set thee free:
And break thy schemes of earthly joy,
That thou mayst seek thy all in Me.'

Becoming like Jesus

These verses helped me to realize that many of my problems and difficulties actually were God's answer to my prayer to be made more Christlike.

As we love someone increasingly we desire to please that person. As our love for God deepens so our desire to serve him increases.

How then can we who have known a measure of pain, hurt and disappointment in our lives best serve God?

David Watson's words are helpful:

> A chef will beat a steak before he cooks it in order to make it tender, likewise, because sin creates in us a hardness of heart, God may take us through many painful experiences in order to make us tender hearted and compassionate, like His son. When our hearts are made tender through suffering we may find an enriched ministry towards those who suffer. (David Watson, *Discipleship,* Hodder & Stoughton 1981, p.254.)

Our own suffering increases our sensitivity to others who are suffering. Only those who have experienced hurt can help those who are hurting.

There is no need to look far in our churches and in the world around us, to find people who are bruised and battered by life's experiences. Many are desperately looking for an individual who will stretch out a loving and understanding hand to support them. We who have known personal pain may be able to share with them the ways in which God has helped us. Paul talks of God as the one 'who comforts us in all our troubles, so that we can comfort those in any trouble with the comfort we ourselves have received from God' (2 Corinthians 1:4).

A whole world of need

If we allow God to use our situations to make us tender rather than bitter, understanding rather than resentful, outgoing and outward-looking rather than inward-looking and self-pitying, then we will discover a whole world of need surrounding us in which God wants to use us. Ours can be the privilege of helping others in need.

One childless couple we know well have had their lives enriched by reaching out to students in their church who are homesick and lonely. They chat to them and have them home for meals and relaxation and are able to give of themselves to a degree that would be impossible if there were family needs to be attended to.

Other couples, because of their ability to be more involved in the work of the church, have been a great source of encouragement to their minister and strength to the church.

What about those who are not married? Childless couples have areas in common with them. They struggle with their desire for a marriage partner and with God's denial of this. Churches often expect a lot from single people but give little in return. Couples without children would have a particular contribution to make in friendships with these single people.

We need churches who care for those within the church as well as for those outside. We need homes where people in need know and feel Christian love. Yet churches often appear to be so family-orientated that there seems to be little place for the single, the childless, the divorced or the widowed (the very ones God singles out as in need of special care).

Some couples find their church difficult because of a family emphasis which makes them feel excluded.

Enriching experience

To admit in some Christian circles to being lonely, depressed or unable to cope is to admit to being weak. This is equated with spiritual immaturity. Yet such intolerance of weakness is not shared by Jesus or the writers of the epistles. Many of God's greatest servants have suffered from depression, discouragement and loneliness at times; men like Spurgeon, David Brainerd and John Bunyan. What of Elijah, David and Paul? It is through weakness that we learn dependence on God, and learn how to draw on his strength. From the beginning of time God has used suffering to mould and develop his servants, fitting them for his kingdom and service. We can be encouraged to realize that God loves us enough to bother about what we are like!

Our concern must not be about how many times or how hard God tests us but rather about our response to it. As Paul writes: 'We are hard pressed on every side, but not crushed; perplexed, but not in despair; persecuted, but not abandoned; struck down, but not destroyed' (2 Corinthians 4:8–9).

As I look back now and remember particular times of pain and sadness, I have no regrets. I can now readily admit that being childless has proved to be one of the most enriching experiences of my life.

I have often been forced to re-examine my position as a Christian. When you are in agony inside yourself you cannot be an armchair Christian or an apathetic follower of Christ. Either God becomes very real to you or you give up.

I am glad God has made himself real to me.